Pelican Books
# Unemployment

Kevin Hawkins was educated at Keighley Grammar School and Gonville
and Caius College, Cambridge, where he gained a double first-class
honours degree. He holds three research degrees, including a Ph.D.
obtained in 1981. From 1970 to 1982 he was lecturer in Industrial
Relations at the University of Bradford Management Centre, and then
he joined the CBI as Director of its West Midlands region. In 1984 he
was appointed Director of Public Affairs for Lucas Industries plc. He has
extensive experience of management consultancy, particularly in the
field of training and development, and also of local government. He was
a member of Bradford Metropolitan Council from 1975 to 1983. His
most recent publications include *The Management of Industrial Relations*
(Pelican, 1978), *Unemployment* (Pelican, of which this book is a completely revised edition), *A Handbook of Industrial Relations Practice* (1979),
*Trade Unions* (1981) and *Case Studies in Industrial Relations* (1982).

KEVIN HAWKINS

# UNEMPLOYMENT

*Third Edition*

PENGUIN BOOKS

Penguin Books Ltd, Harmondsworth, Middlesex, England
Viking Penguin Inc., 40 West 23rd Street, New York, New York 10010, U.S.A.
Penguin Books Australia Ltd, Ringwood, Victoria, Australia
Penguin Books Canada Limited, 2801 John Street, Markham, Ontario, Canada L3R 1B4
Penguin Books (N.Z.) Ltd, 182–190 Wairau Road, Auckland 10, New Zealand

First published 1979
Second edition 1984
Third edition 1987

Made and printed in Great Britain by
Richard Clay Ltd, Bungay, Suffolk
Filmset in Monophoto Photina

# CONTENTS

# PREFACE

Looking back to the Preface to the first edition of this book, which was written in May 1979 against a background of roughly 1·3 million registered unemployed, I find the following words: 'It seems certain, therefore, that over the next two or three years aggregate unemployment will rise once again, probably to new postwar heights, as the economy adjusts both to the government's strategy and to the projected recession in world trade.' In common with most other observers, however, I did not anticipate that unemployment would more than double during the ensuing recession nor that it would continue to rise, if more slowly, during the subsequent cyclical recovery. We all underestimated the loss of competitiveness which British industry sustained during the 1970s (as, indeed, did most politicians) and therefore took an unduly optimistic view of the ability of the economy as a whole to generate more employment. In the Preface to the second edition of this book, written in August 1983, I therefore emphasized that a long-term strategy for assisting the creation of employment throughout the economy depends crucially on the performance of the manufacturing sector. It is regrettable, therefore, to note in introducing the third edition of this book that this message has yet to be fully accepted by those who currently control or influence government policy. In the meantime the current level of unemployment has become *the* political issue of the day and a major vote-loser for any government which appears powerless to reduce it.

Not that governments, of whatever political colour, *can* do much to cut unemployment substantially in the short term – which is, of course, the politician's normal time horizon. From what we know of the likely trend in the number of people seeking to enter the labour market, and what we fear may be the overall growth rate of the economy, it requires no particular prescience to predict that total registered unemployment will almost certainly remain above 3 million and could rise to nearer 4 million over the next few years. This implies a further increase in the proportion of people on the register who have been jobless for twelve months or more. It does not, however, imply a fatalistic belief that little can be done beyond what is already being done to frustrate this prediction. The starting point is to grasp the unpalatable truth that much of the unemployment in Britain today is structural in origin and is therefore unlikely to be reduced to any great extent either by the conventional tools of monetary and fiscal policy, or by cyclical growth in the economy, or by eliminating 'scroungers' from the unemployment register. Structural problems require structural solutions, which implies a longer-term perspective than policy-makers have so far been inclined to adopt.

I should like to thank Mrs Madelyn Coyne for assisting me in preparing the present text. The opinions expressed in it are, of course, essentially my own and not necessarily those of Lucas Industries plc.

Kevin Hawkins
May 1986

# CHAPTER 1

# LIVING WITH HIGH UNEMPLOYMENT

*Employment cannot be created by Act of Parliament or by Government action alone. Government policy will be directed to bringing about conditions favourable to the maintenance of a high level of employment ... But the success of the policy outlined in this Paper will ultimately depend on the understanding and support of the community as a whole and especially on the efforts of employers and workers in industry, for without a rising standard of industrial efficiency we cannot achieve a high level of employment combined with a rising standard of living.*

White Paper on Employment Policy, 1944

For thirty years after these words were written, British society as a whole regarded full employment as the normal state of affairs. While the authors of the 1944 White Paper referred to 'high' employment, the actual performance of the postwar British economy seemed to suggest that they had been unduly cautious. Sir William (later Lord) Beveridge, popularly regarded as the intellectual father of full employment, defined a fully employed society as one in which 'those who lose jobs must be able to find new jobs at fair wages within their capacity without delay'.[1] This definition implied that at any given time those who registered as unemployed would simply be 'between jobs' and the number of people in this category should not, said Beveridge, average more than 550,000 people, or roughly 3 per cent of the labour force.[2] Up to the mid-1960s, however, the average number of people on the unemployment register in the United Kingdom was about 350,000, or rather less than 2 per cent of the labour force. Despite a slight increase in unemployment during the late 1960s, and a rather sharper increase during the recession of 1970–72, economists continued to debate whether a greater margin of 'slack' in the labour market might not be preferable to the reality of excessive inflation.[3]

Subsequent experience has, in effect, stood Beveridge on his head. Not only is aggregate unemployment currently (spring 1986) running at more than four times the level defined by Beveridge as 'full' employment, but – equally important – the other key elements in his definition are little more than historical curiosities. Full employment, he argued, meant 'having more vacancies for workers than there are workers seeking vacancies', so that unemployment 'would be reduced to short intervals of standing by' and no one would be 'demoralised' by long periods of enforced idleness.[4] In fact, however, as early as the 1960s nearly one-third of those on the unemployment register were likely to have been out of work for more than six months. During the 1970s this proportion steadily rose and increased sharply in the recession of 1979–82. By mid-1985 some 18 per cent of the total number of unemployed men had been on the register between six months and a year, while no less than 46 per cent had been there for over a year.

Beveridge's requirements on both wages and personal capacity have also been overtaken by the changing realities of the labour market. Over the past decade or so one of the most important tenets of classical economics has become firmly embodied in official thinking and policy – namely that the level of employment is largely, if not exclusively, determined by the price of labour. In the words of a recent White Paper 'Jobs will be created to the extent that people are prepared to work at wages that employers can afford.'[5] A major cause of the rise in unemployment, in other words, is that workers – aided by strong trade unions – have priced themselves out of the labour market. The idea that the unemployed should expect to get alternative jobs at 'fair' wages has, therefore, been firmly displaced by the older conviction that such jobs will only materialize if workers will accept the 'market-clearing' level of pay in return. By the same token, the kind of jobs on offer are less and less matched with the personal capabilities of the unemployed because the economy is changing and, with it, the structure of employment. It is, therefore, unrealistic for most people who find themselves without a job to expect new jobs to be provided which do not require either personal mobility or the acquisition of new skills, or frequently both.

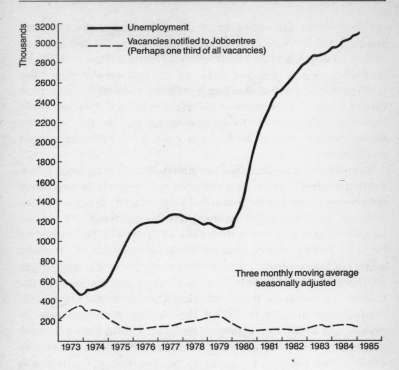

Figure 1   (Source: *Employment Gazette*, April 1987.)

Not only has Beveridge's concept of full employment been
effectively destroyed by the experience of the past decade, the
policy framework which was once thought capable of ensuring
that this ideal remained a practical reality has also lost much of
its credibility. Beveridge and a generation of postwar politicians
with vivid memories of the 1930s shared a conviction that mass
unemployment not only should but could be avoided in future.
While the total mobilization of the economy had resolved the
problem of unemployment during wartime, the work of J. M.
Keynes had shown governments how they could maintain full
employment in peacetime. In *The General Theory of Employment,
Interest and Money* (1936), Keynes attacked the orthodox, classical doctrine that there was an automatic tendency in a competitive economy towards a full employment equilibrium. An

economy could, he argued, get stuck at the trough of a recession due to a deficiency in *aggregate demand*. The level of demand was held to be dependent on investment and consumption and if these two components did not add up to full employment, the government could fill the gap by either reducing taxation or raising its own expenditure. An expansion in total demand would increase prices relative to money wages and in this way the labour market would be brought back to a full employment equilibrium.

Keynesian ideas broadly dominated British economic policy until the early 1970s. The declared policy goals of successive governments were to maintain full employment, to achieve price stability, to encourage economic growth and to achieve a satisfactory balance of trade with the rest of the world. Unfortunately British industry proved itself increasingly incapable of attaining a level of international competitiveness which would have made all these goals achievable. An underlying deterioration in the balance of payments from the mid-1950s onwards forced successive governments to defend the sterling exchange rate by periodically depressing aggregate demand. This in turn held back the rate of economic growth without reversing the underlying tendency for inflation to increase. Incomes policy – which was meant to hold down inflation without sacrificing full (or reasonably full) employment – proved to be ineffective in an economy with an increasingly decentralized system of pay determination. Fixed exchange rates were finally abandoned at the beginning of the 1970s and thereafter full employment gave way to curbing inflation as the overriding objective of economic policy. Faith in Keynesian demand management was already badly eroded when Prime Minister James Callaghan openly attacked it in 1976: 'We used to think that you could just spend your way out of a recession and increase employment by cutting taxes and reducing government spending. I tell you, in all candour, that that option no longer exists and that insofar as it ever did exist, it only worked on each occasion since the war by injecting bigger doses of inflation into the economy, followed by higher levels of unemployment at the next step.'[6] The growth of unemployment was seen as the direct consequence of past excesses – particularly in wage bargaining. It could only be halted and reversed by a combination of hard work, greater efficiency and sustained self-discipline on the part of the workforce.

The extent to which this view, with its strong puritan overtones, has become generally accepted over the past decade helps to explain the apparent ambiguity of public attitudes to unemployment. On the one hand successive opinion polls suggest a high level of anxiety among the public at large about the current level of unemployment and a strong desire to see it reduced. Leaving aside humanitarian considerations, many people are aware of the waste of resources and the huge cost to the public purse (currently equivalent to over 2 per cent of GDP) of unemployment benefit. Government ministers and Conservative Members of Parliament, particularly those representing marginal urban constituencies, clearly regard unemployment as a vote-loser and wish to be seen to be 'doing something about it'. On the other hand there is also a popular belief that a significant number of the unemployed are better off financially on the dole than they would be if they were working, that others are drawing an acceptable living from the black economy and that many of the remainder are virtually unemployable. Meanwhile economists and politicians continue to offer conflicting 'solutions' to the problem in a context where faith in the policies of the past has been virtually destroyed by the experience of the 1970s.

In the course of this book we shall attempt to chart a path through these conflicting arguments and assess the prospects for reducing the current level of unemployment. Since, however, public discussion of this topic tends to be dominated by the official unemployment statistics and since there are still some misconceptions about the meaning of these figures and the technical terms which surround them, it is this topic which must first be discussed.

## CLASSIFYING UNEMPLOYMENT

It is customary to distinguish between three types of unemployment – *frictional*, *structural* and *cyclical* – and this clas-
sification will be used here for convenience. This does not, of
course, mean that one or another of these labels can be un-
ambiguously applied to specific individuals on the unemployment
register. They are somewhat arbitrary, shorthand terms which
together provide an approach both to analysing the reasons why
workers became unemployed and to formulating strategies to
reduce unemployment.

*Frictional* unemployment arises when workers change their
jobs but are obliged, because of a lack of instant interchangeability and mobility, to spend a short time (less than, say,
two months) on the unemployment register. There are in fact
some eight or nine million job changes every year and with a
turnover of this size some short-term unemployment is virtually
inevitable. The frictionally unemployed are, by definition, those
for whom jobs exist: 'These jobs are reasonably suited to the
skills of the unemployed, are within reach of their homes and
are at current rates of pay. It follows ... that frictional unemployment can only exist alongside an unsatisfied demand for
labour.'[7] If frictional unemployment is increasing it may be
because the general demand for labour is high or rising so that
workers are encouraged to change their jobs. Alternatively, it
may indicate that, irrespective of the general level of demand,
there is a growing mismatch between the skills, aptitudes and
characteristics of the unemployed and the requirements of employers as expressed in vacancies. In neither case, however,
would the remedy lie in stimulating the general demand for
labour. Indeed, it has been argued that, since 'changing jobs is a
desirable process both for the individual and society', frictional
unemployment should be regarded as relatively costless and even
beneficial.[8] It is misleading, however, to portray this type of
unemployment as exclusively voluntary in character. A skilled
worker who is dismissed by reason of redundancy, for example,
may find another job within two months but could hardly be
described as voluntarily unemployed.

*Structural* unemployment is commonly seen as a more extreme type of frictional unemployment insofar as it implies a mismatch between the characteristics of the unemployed and the jobs that are available in the local labour market. In Cheshire's words, 'Structural unemployment consists of those for whom there are no vacancies in their own categories in the region but for whom there would be vacancies if they could change their category.'[9] As such it is most likely to occur in areas or towns dominated by a declining industry. A closely related but distinct type of unemployment has been labelled *structuralist*. This draws attention to the effects on unemployment of the long-term decline of manufacturing industry and the growth of the service sector, trends characteristic of most Western countries. The most striking effect of this structural change has been a sharp and sustained rise in the unemployed rate of unskilled male manual workers relative to the general rate. This trend has been identified in virtually every region of the UK and may help to account for the relatively narrow dispersion of regional unemployment rates which now prevails compared with that of the inter-war years.[10] It may also help to explain the growth of long-term unemployment in the UK since the 1950s. The fact, however, that this trend is attributable to fundamental structural changes in the economy which have occurred and will continue to occur at any level of aggregate demand suggests that the remedy, if there is one, will be found in policies designed to improve the supply side of the labour market.

*Cyclical* unemployment is directly attributable to the economic cycle and as such was recognized by pre-Keynesian economists: 'This fluctuation of industrial activity has clearly nothing to do with the wishes or characteristics of the men employed. It is not within the control of individual employers. It is not limited to particular trades. It represents alternate expansion and contraction in the demand for labour . . .'[11] In Keynesian terminology such unemployment is caused by a deficiency in aggregate demand, i.e. when total expenditures in an economy are insufficient to generate jobs for all those willing to work at the equilibrium wage.[12] It is generally agreed that in most Western economies deficiency of aggregate demand was rarely experienced during the postwar period up to the oil crisis of 1973. Demand and output continued to increase over the period as a whole with only relatively minor fluctuations around the underlying or trend rate of growth. In Britain's case the main components of high demand were private investment and exports.[13] Since 1973, however, the growth of demand has fallen below its previous trend rate, leading to an increased margin of spare productive capacity and higher unemployment in the UK and elsewhere.

The recovery from the 'oil shock' of 1973–4 was generally slow and average unemployment in Western Europe remained significantly higher than it had been in the 1960s. The second 'oil shock' of 1978–80 precipitated another and more severe world recession, compounded in Britain by the government's refusal to adopt job-creating counter-cyclical measures such as tax reductions or large-scale expenditure on public works. Successive CBI surveys reported that 'lack of demand' was by far the biggest constraint on industrial output – a trend which continued well into the slow cyclical upturn of 1982–5. In this sense it is possible to argue that the bulk of current unemployment is due to a deficiency in aggregate demand. Yet despite an increase of over 11 per cent in Britain's GDP between mid-1981 and mid-1985, unemployment continued to grow, albeit at a much more modest rate than before. This suggests that structural changes in the economy, particularly the decline in manufacturing employment, may have raised the long-run rate of unemployment.

It would, of course, be misleading to assume that demand-deficient and non demand-deficient unemployment exist independently of each other, especially in the context of the recent recession. Male manual workers who are increasingly affected by structural unemployment, for example, are even less likely to get jobs if demand in the economy as a whole is depressed. By the same token, a strong upswing in demand will not resolve the structural unemployment which is now an obvious feature of many inner-city areas but it may slow down the growth of such unemployment as marginal firms find themselves able to continue in business. Nevertheless it would be reasonable to assume that in recent years some unemployment has been the result of inadequate demand and some would have occurred even if demand had been higher. A more detailed analysis of the reasons why unemployment has increased since 1973 is presented below.

## MEASURING UNEMPLOYMENT: THE STOCK

Up to November 1982, when the counting system was changed, the unemployment statistics covered all those unemployed persons who were registered at the Department of Employment as seeking work, being capable of work and available for work, whether they were entitled to unemployment benefit or not. On a certain day in every month each employment office submitted a head count of all those who happened to be on the register on that particular day. When added together these monthly returns made up the total or 'stock' figure for unemployment, which hit the newspaper headlines with unfailing regularity. Since November 1982 the basis of the monthly statistics has been a computerized count of those people who are entitled to unemployment benefit. The main effect of this change has been to reduce the total stock of unemployed by about 6 per cent – a variation which is hardly significant for the purposes of our analysis.

In 1985 the average stock figure of unemployment in the UK was 3·2 million, or just over 13 per cent of the labour force. It is generally agreed, however, that these stock figures are not and never have been 'perfect indicators either of the demand for labour or of social distress'.[14] On the one hand it has been argued that they *understate* the true level of unemployment because at any given time there are always a large number of people who are looking for work but who do not claim unemployment benefit because they are not eligible – for example, women whose husbands have jobs. According to the government's annual Labour Force Survey, in the spring of 1984 this group totalled 870,000. Some commentators also insist on adding in the 600,000 or so people who are currently employed on the various

government-financed special employment programmes, including the Youth Training Scheme, on the ground that virtually
all of them would otherwise be on the register.

On the other hand it is also the case that the monthly count
*exaggerates* the real level of unemployment because it includes a
large group of people who, although claiming benefits, are
'economically inactive'. In the spring of 1984 this group totalled
940,000, of whom some 200,000 had a paid job and the remainder were not actively seeking work at the time of the survey.
Are these the 'welfare scroungers' of popular repute? The Department of Employment has always urged caution when
interpreting these figures. In the 1984 survey 28 per cent of
these 740,000 economically inactive claimants gave as their
reason for not seeking work a belief that no jobs were available
for them. It would therefore be best to describe them as 'discouraged workers' – people who are likely to have been unemployed for long periods of time and whose previous attempts
to find work have been unsuccessful. Of the remainder, some 17
per cent classed themselves as long-term sick or disabled, 26
per cent (mainly women) said they were looking after the
home and 8 per cent were retired. Those who said that they
did not want or need a job formed a small minority (7 per
cent) of both male and female inactive claimants. The Department of Employment also points out that many of the people
classed as inactive, and not necessarily just those who were
'discouraged', may have genuinely wished to work given the
opportunity, but were not actively looking for work at the time
of the survey.

On balance, therefore, it seems likely that the stock figures
based on the monthly count marginally understate the real level
of unemployment.


MEASURING UNEMPLOYMENT: THE FLOW

Irrespective of how far the monthly count can be revised upwards
or downwards, the most misleading characteristic of the stock
figure is the impression it gives of a steadily deepening but

otherwise stagnant pool of unemployed. Another false analogy is that of a rubbish-tip, the height of which increases as unemployment rises and workers of progressively higher quality are 'shaken out' by redundancy. A more realistic image would be that of a bath constantly being filled from a tap of 'joiners' and emptied through a plug-hole for 'leavers'. In a recession the tap flows faster than the plug-hole can discharge, so that the level of 'water' rises, but there is always a significant outflow. The net difference between these large flows on to and off the register represents the relatively small movement in the stock figure reported from the monthly count. Since 1973 between 280,000 and 420,000 men and women have joined the register *every month* and a slightly higher or lower figure has left it, depending on the general level of demand for labour:

Table 1   The stock and flow of unemployment, 1973–85

|  | 1973 | 1977 | 1981 | 1985 |
| --- | --- | --- | --- | --- |
| Average monthly flow on to register | 284,000 | 292,000 | 334,000 | 419,000 |
| Average monthly flow off register | 304,000 | 286,000 | 277,000 | 388,000 |
| Total number of unemployed* | 476,000 | 1,480,000 | 2,940,000 | 3,273,100 |
| Unemployment rate % | 2·1 | 6·2 | 12·3 | 13·5 |
| Number out of work for over 12 months (men only) | 143,000 | 252,000 | 467,000 | 1,044,000 |

* Seasonally adjusted, December stock figure.
(Source: *Employment Gazette*, various issues.)

It will be evident from Table 1 that the monthly inflow in general contributes little to the total stock. Between December 1973 and December 1981, for example, the total number of unemployed increased six-fold, but the flow into unemployment rose by only

17·6 per cent. The crucial factor is the length of time which each unemployed person spends on the register. A slight increase in the median length of completed spells of unemployment can have a disproportionate effect on the monthly stock figure. Indeed, Daniel has suggested that the stock level is best seen as a rough-and-ready indicator of the length of time it takes the unemployed to find work.[15] In the 1960s about half of those who became unemployed left the register within two weeks of joining it; by the mid-1970s about half were leaving within one month and 90 per cent within six months.[16] Daniel has estimated that in 1981 the median duration was three to four months, with about one-third of the total stock leaving within a month.

Since 1981 turnover on the register has remained high, with over 4 million individuals entering and leaving unemployment each year. The total monthly inflow has, however, been increasing since the late 1970s due to the growing propensity of women to register and the sharp contraction of manufacturing employment during the recent recession – a process which is still continuing. As the growth of alternative employment opportunities has not kept pace with the inflow on to the register, so the median length of stay on the register has doubled and long-term unemployment has increased accordingly:

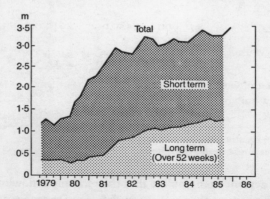

Figure 2   Long-term unemployment in the UK, 1979–85. (Source: *Employment Gazette*.)

Nevertheless, the majority of workers who join the register at any given time can reasonably anticipate that they will leave it within weeks or months rather than stay there permanently.

## THE STOCK AND FLOW OF VACANCIES

Data on the flow of vacancies is a useful complement to that on unemployment insofar as it represents, albeit imperfectly, a measure of the demand for labour. Its major weakness is that it represents less than half, and perhaps as little as one-third, of the total number of vacancies in the economy at any given time since employers may advertise vacancies without notifying them to the Employment Service. Nevertheless, registered unemployment and vacancies are both related to the level of economic activity and so to each other (see Figure 2). As with unemployment, the monthly flow figures are more stable than the stock levels and the time taken to fill vacancies is therefore the key variable in explaining changes in the level. The higher the level of unemployment, the faster will most vacancies be filled and vice versa. In general, however, there are relatively few vacancies which cannot be filled quickly. Even in 1979, when both the inflow and the stock of vacancies was relatively high, half were filled within two working days and three-quarters within five working days.[17]

This rapid turnover must be borne in mind when considering the oft-heard claim that, despite the level of unemployment, there are still a large number of vacancies available to those workers who are prepared to go out and look for them, move house or undergo retraining. The fact that unemployment can exist alongside persistent labour shortages is usually quoted in support of the argument that many of the unemployed, cushioned by generous welfare benefits, have become too choosy in accepting work and have acquired unrealistic expectations. It is certainly true that the unemployment–vacancy ratio has changed since the mid-1960s so that a given stock of vacancies has been associated with a higher level of unemployment. But this rightward shift in the U/V curve is largely attributable to the growing

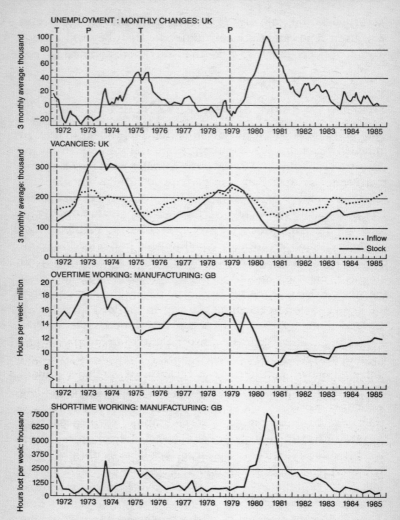

Figure 3   Labour   market   indicators.   (Source:   *Employment   Gazette*,
November 1985.)

tendency – first noted in 1966 – for employers facing low or falling demand to 'shake out' surplus labour rather than hoard it.[18] In other words, the upward trend in unemployment, particularly among men, is primarily due to the decline in employment, especially in manufacturing industry, rather than to an allegedly growing reluctance on the part of the unemployed to accept what is available. The stock of vacancies is not a stagnant pool of jobs waiting to be filled by the unemployed – on the contrary, the turnover is rapid.

There are of course a significant number of vacancies which are difficult to fill, but these tend to be jobs which are not easily matched with the characteristics of most unemployed people. The most persistent 'hard to fill' vacancies which have been reported over the past decade or more are engineering craftsmen and related types of skilled labour, particularly in the south-east. Problems have also been reported in filling vacancies in certain service-sector occupations such as catering, nursing and hairdressing. In such cases the reasons include unattractive pay and conditions, unsocial hours and a lack of suitably qualified applicants.

In addition many manufacturing firms throughout the country have recently complained of the difficulty of recruiting electronics engineers and information technologists. Many such vacancies are not only hard to fill but hard to *keep* filled, as employers tend to poach key skilled workers from each other. The solution to this problem, however, lies not so much in the need for more mobility and flexibility among the unemployed as in changes to the national system of education and training which will increase the output of suitably qualified manpower.

## INTERNATIONAL PERSPECTIVES

Before concluding this introductory section we need to place Britain's current unemployment problem in some kind of international perspective. It is frequently pointed out that rising unemployment is not a phenomenon unique to Britain and that, by implication, it is unrealistic to think in terms of a purely national solution. A relatively small economy on the periphery of Europe cannot 'fine tune' its way back to full employment unless the rest of the world in general, and its major trading partners in particular, are moving in the same overall direction. At present, however, this is clearly not the case.

In Western Europe as a whole unemployment rose from 4 per cent of the workforce in 1979 to around 11 per cent in 1984. Taking the OECD as a whole, approximately 31 million people are currently unemployed and there is no optimism that this total can be significantly reduced, at least in the short term. Having said this, it is clear from Figures 3 and 4 that since 1979 not only has unemployment risen faster in Britain than in other major industrial economies, but that Britain's performance in creating new employment to offset the lost jobs has also been relatively poor. Within the rise in total unemployment there has also been a general increase in joblessness among young people and a growth in long-term unemployment among all groups of the labour force. Here again, Britain's performance has been significantly worse than that of any other major OECD economy except France. Consequently, in seeking to explain why unemployment generally has increased and is likely to remain at historically high levels in most industrialized countries, we also need to explore why the British experience has been significantly worse than the average.

## SUMMARY

While the official unemployment returns marginally understate the real level of unemployment, the flow on to and off the register is still relatively rapid and the image of a rubbish tip or stagnant pool of unemployed is generally misleading. The majority of the unemployed are likely to stay on the register for a few weeks or months and unemployment is for them a 'hiatus' rather than a state or condition. Similarly, although the official statistics on vacancies cover only about a third of the jobs available at any given time, turnover on this register is also rapid and the number of hard-to-fill vacancies remains a small minority of the total.

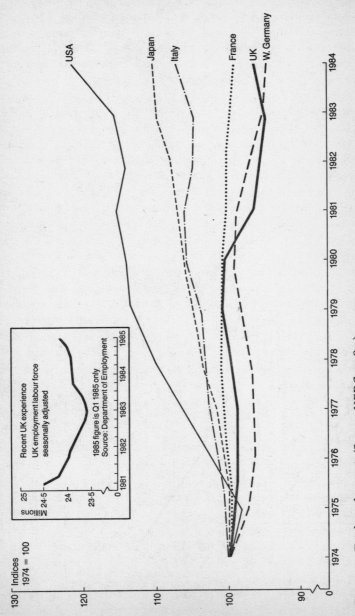

Figure 4   Total employment. (Source: NEDC, 1985.)

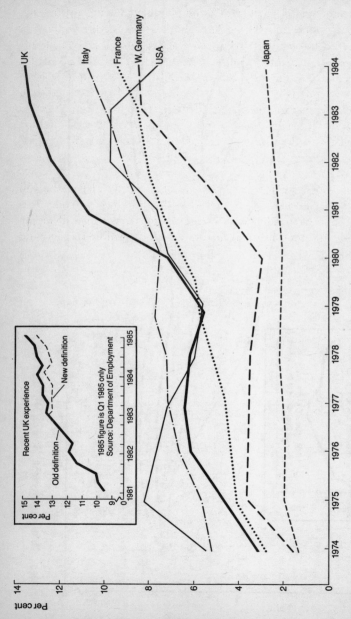

Figure 5  Unemployment: Percentage of total labour force. (Source: NEDC, 1985.)

The experience of short-term unemployment lasting up to, say, six months may not be particularly pleasant for the individual concerned, but at least those who move into and out of un-employment fairly quickly are, by definition, active and successful job-seekers. It is for these reasons that the growth of long-term unemployment in Britain, as elsewhere, must be regarded as a particularly disturbing trend. If there *is* a stagnant pool or rubbish-tip of unemployed people, we are most likely to find it among those who have been out of work for over a year. Sugges-tions for reducing the size of this group will be discussed later in this book.

Total unemployment in Britain is significantly higher than in most other comparable countries. In order to discover why this should be so we need to look first at changes in the overall supply of labour and then at those factors which determine the demand for labour.

# CHAPTER 2

# THE LABOUR MARKET: SUPPLY

*The problem of unemployment is the problem of the adjustment of the supply of labour and the demand for labour . . . Discrepancy between two things so distinct in immediate origin is obviously possible. The problem has merely to be stated in order to shatter the simple faith that at all times any man who really wants work can obtain it. There is nothing in the existing industrial order to secure this miraculously perfect adjustment.*

W. H. Beveridge, 1909

Unemployment has risen in most Western countries because the working population has expanded more rapidly than employment opportunities. This somewhat trite but none the less true statement focuses attention on those factors which determine the size and composition of the labour force. If the labour force – those people of working age who are either employed or seeking work – is expanding more rapidly than the job-creating capabilities of industrial economies, then the long-run rate of unemployment must be rising. The appropriate policy response would therefore involve measures to improve the rate of job creation and simultaneously ensure that the characteristics of those seeking work were more closely matched with the requirements of employers. A complementary strategy, given the size of the problem, would be to seek marginal reductions in the labour supply, largely by encouraging some people either to withdraw from the labour market or not to enter it at all. Another supply-side influence on the underlying trend in unemployment is the 'shock absorber' provided by unemployment and related benefits. If this is now strong enough to induce some people to substitute unemployment for work, or voluntarily withhold their labour, then unemployment will tend to rise. The appropriate policy response would therefore be to reduce the real level of benefits relative to the income which people could expect to receive if they were in work.

## THE WORKING POPULATION

The working population of Great Britain currently stands at about 27·4 million, comprising 21·2 million employees in employment, 2·6 million employers and self-employed, 326,000 members of HM Forces and 3·3 million unemployed. The total is roughly 4 million more than in 1951 and one million more than in 1975. Changes in its size are determined by two variables – the size of the population which is of working age, and the proportion of the working-age population who participate in the labour force (the 'activity rate'). In recent years the population of working age has been increasing quite strongly. This is the result of a low average level of retirement, itself the consequence of low birth rates during the First World War, and a sharp rise in the number of teenagers due to the high birth rates of the 1960s. Activity rates differ between demographic groups and for any given group may change over time. Among all *men*, for example, there is a long-run tendency for activity rates to decline, although short-term fluctuations seem to occur in response to variations in employment opportunities. Activity rates among *women*, by contrast, have increased sharply over the past forty years or so. In 1950 women constituted about 30 per cent of the labour force, rising to 37 per cent by 1971 and nearly 42 per cent by 1985. Table 2 summarizes the past and projected changes in the labour force, identifying the separate contributions of population and activity-rate effects.

It is immediately clear from Table 2 that between 1977 and 1981 the effect of a rising population on the labour force was greatly reduced by a sharp fall in male activity rates, presumably in response to shrinking employment opportunities. During 1981–3, a much greater fall in male activity rates and a significant decline in female activity rates more than offset the population effect, resulting in a reduction in the labour force. In 1983–4, by contrast, a very sharp recovery in female activity rates

**Table 2  Components of change in the civilian labour force (annual averages)**

*Great Britain*                                                        *Thousand*

| | Male and Female | | |
| --- | --- | --- | --- |
| | Population effect* | Activity-rate effect† | Change in the labour force |
| 1971–7 | 49 | 119 | 168 |
| 1977–81 | 146 | −64 | 82 |
| 1981–3 | 177 | −341 | −164 |
| 1983–4 | 218 | 294 | 512 |
| 1984–9 | 88 | 61 | 149 |
| 1989–91 | 6 | 36 | 42 |

| Male | | | Female | | |
| --- | --- | --- | --- | --- | --- |
| Population effect* | Activity-rate effect† | Change in the labour force | Population effect* | Activity-rate effect† | Change in the labour force |
| 41 | −39 | 2 | 8 | 158 | 166 |
| 81 | −65 | 16 | 65 | 0 | 66 |
| 104 | −250 | −147 | 73 | −91 | −18 |
| 145 | −18 | 127 | 73 | 311 | 385 |
| 58 | 1 | 59 | 30 | 61 | 90 |
| 14 | −3 | 10 | −7 | 39 | 32 |

* The change in the labour force that would have occurred had the activity rate in each age group remained over the period at its value in the initial year.
† The residual change – the total change less the population effect.
(Source: *Employment Gazette*, July 1983.)

combined with stronger population effects for both men and women to produce a substantial rise in the labour force. Consequently the upturn in employment opportunities which induced the rise in female activity rates was insufficient to absorb the growth in the labour force and total unemployment rose slightly among both men and women. Unemployment would in fact have

risen more strongly in 1983–4 had there not also been an increase of about 400,000 in the number of self-employed people
during this period.

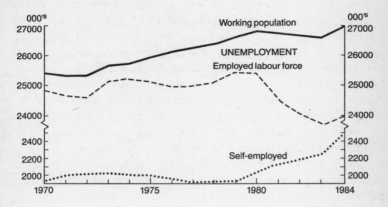

Figure 6   Employment and unemployment, 1970–84. (Source: *Employment Gazette*, various issues.)

Was it inevitable that the large increase in the population of
working age which has occurred in the UK since the mid-1970s
should have produced higher unemployment? It has been pointed
out that during the 1930s the economy comfortably absorbed a
9 per cent increase in the population of working age and simultaneously reduced unemployment by half. It has also been
observed that since 1975 the UK has had a *lower* rate of working-
age population growth than virtually any other OECD country.
It cannot, therefore, be argued that it is the growth of Britain's
potential labour supply which is responsible for the rise in unemployment.[1]

Do changing activity rates among men and women help to
explain the growth of unemployment? The most conspicuous
feature of the growth in the UK labour force since 1971 has
been the entry of increased numbers of women into the labour
market. Between 1971 and 1985 the male labour force fell by
about 90,000 and at no time in the intervening period was it
more than 0·5 per cent above the level of 1971. The female
labour force, by contrast, grew by 1·6 million, or about 17 per

cent, over the same period. This growth in female activity rates is not, however, peculiar to Britain, where the current rate for women is not significantly at variance with those of other comparable countries – particularly in the prime age groups between twenty-five and fifty-four years. This trend may have been influenced by certain supply-side factors such as declining family sizes, the development of a more tolerant attitude towards working wives and mothers, and the need for additional income in households where the male bread-winner is unemployed. Indeed it is sometimes claimed that this female invasion of the labour market has resulted in significant *displacement* of male workers and thereby contributed to the rise in male unemployment. This is, however, unlikely.

The most plausible explanation of rising female participation in the labour force is an expansion in employment opportunities for women. These opportunities have come from two sources. Firstly, those industries and services which employ a high ratio of female to male workers have expanded rapidly. Employment in health services, for example, where women heavily outnumber men, grew by 40 per cent between 1971 and 1985. Secondly, there has been a marked growth throughout the economy in part-time employment.[2] Over two-thirds of the jobs created in the service sector since 1971 have been part-time and during the recent cyclical upswing virtually the only type of employment which has increased has been part-time. Britain is unusual not so much in the proportion of women who work part-time (46 per cent) but in the very high proportion of part-time employees – 90 per cent, compared with 70 per cent in the USA – who are women rather than men.[3] A significant growth in part-time employment is likely to benefit women accordingly. Presumably some of these jobs could be done by men, but employers generally seem to prefer to recruit women. The growth of part-time employment for women does not, therefore, explain the general rise in unemployment but it *does* help to account for the fact that in recent years both employment and unemployment have risen together.[4]

Will these trends continue? Current projections by the Department of Employment suggest that demographic pressures will continue to expand the labour force over the next few years.

Between 1984 and 1989 the population of working age is projected to rise by about 440,000. Assuming that there will be no
significant change in the average activity rate for men (about 74
per cent) and that the female activity rate will continue to increase from its current level of nearly 49 per cent to 50 per cent,
the labour force is projected to grow by about 750,000 up to the
end of the decade. It is anticipated that about 60 per cent of this
addition to the labour force will be female. The Department points
out, however, that should the rise in part-time jobs for women
continue at the very rapid rate achieved in 1983–4, it is likely
that more women will be attracted into the labour force.[5] Given
the growing willingness of unemployed women to register as
such, this in itself is likely to maintain or increase the total level
of unemployment – unless, of course, the economy succeeds in
creating more jobs than are currently projected.


## HOURS OF WORK

Another supply-side influence on the labour force is the quantity
of working time actually delivered. A distinction should be drawn
between normal basic hours, normal hours and actual hours of
work. The first term relates to the number of hours an employee
is expected to work at basic rates of pay; the second includes any
guaranteed overtime paid at premium rates; the third includes
all overtime, whether guaranteed or not.

In most advanced industrial economies there is a long-run
trend towards a shorter working week, whether measured in
terms of normal or actual hours. Nevertheless it is conceivable
that unemployment has risen because those in employment have
maintained their hours of work at a higher level than might
otherwise have been the case. Back in 1978, for example, the
Department of Employment calculated that if normal weekly
hours in Britain were cut to thirty-five, and there were corresponding reductions in weekly earnings (implying a fall in overtime),
registered unemployment would be reduced by 'anywhere between 100,000 and 500,000'.[6]

In fact, however, there is no evidence to support the view that hours of work in Britain have been held up to the detriment of the unemployed. Up to the late 1960s normal hours fell more rapidly than actual hours, implying an increase in overtime working. Since then, however, normal hours have declined only slightly whereas overtime working, although fluctuating with the economic cycle, has fallen significantly (see Figure 3). The main reasons for the downward trend in actual hours worked include the growth in part-time employment, shorter working weeks and longer holidays. Nor is there any evidence to suggest that other industrial economies have reduced their hours of work more rapidly than Britain. On the contrary, the British working week is now on average shorter than in West Germany and considerably shorter than in the United States and Japan – all countries which currently have relatively lower rates of unemployment.

## IS CURRENT UNEMPLOYMENT VOLUNTARY?

One still encounters the argument, though perhaps less frequently nowadays than during the 1970s, that many workers have chosen of their own free will to be unemployed because they are better off financially out of work than in work. Although easy to dismiss as 'scroungermania', this view has an eminently respectable academic pedigree. Economists in the classical or neoclassical tradition assert that unemployment is due to excessively high real wages and that equilibrium can only be restored if jobs are 'priced back' into the market. Unemployment benefit, however, subsidizes leisure and thereby encourages workers to quit their jobs voluntarily in order to search for better-paid employment. In Minford's words:

For an equilibrium model, unemployment is voluntary. Given unemployment compensation, it may pay people, faced with an unpleasant change in the environment (a drop in the demand for their skills), to remain unemployed rather than move house or change occupation or make whatever changes are required in order to fill the jobs available. Their decision may be to remain unemployed for a longer period (e.g., given the chances that the economy may recover in such a way as to restore the old type of job, they may decide not to take an interim job) or to become *permanently* unemployed because available jobs are just not attractive enough. The UK social security system gives indefinite and generous support in a way that sharply undercuts up to half of the economy's available jobs ... It is probably only habit, the desire to avoid upheaval, and the knowledge that the system must surely be changed in time, which prevent many more people from actually abandoning their existing jobs, rather than simply not making active efforts to find new ones.[7]

If, therefore, it can be shown that a significant amount of unemployment is indeed voluntary, the best way to reduce it would be to cut the real value of social benefits and weaken the power of trade unions to raise relative wages.

Changes in the level of unemployment benefits relative to income from working could undoubtedly influence the long-run rate of unemployment. A rise in the ratio of benefits to earnings, or 'replacement ratio', could induce some workers to leave their jobs and join the register or, more plausibly, to stay on the register if they are already there. The evidence from annual Family Expenditure Surveys suggests that the average benefit/earnings ratio for a potential thirteen-week spell of unemployment rose slightly over the decade 1968–78 to 81 per cent, and for a quarter of the population the ratio was 90 per cent. Between 1978 and 1983, however, the average ratio fell from 81 to 60 per cent as a result of policy changes affecting the level and real value of unemployment benefits.[8] In theory this trend should have induced some workers to substitute jobs for unemployment when in fact, of course, total unemployment doubled.

It is occasionally claimed that Britain is more generous towards its unemployed than other comparable countries and that this helps to explain why British unemployment is relatively high. In fact there is no evidence to support this assertion.

The data represented in Figure 7 suggest that even at the end of the 1970s, *before* the reduction in the average replacement ratio took full effect, Britain was not significantly out of line with France and West Germany in its provision of support for the unemployed who were low paid when in work and was in fact rather less generous in its treatment of those in the higher-income groups.

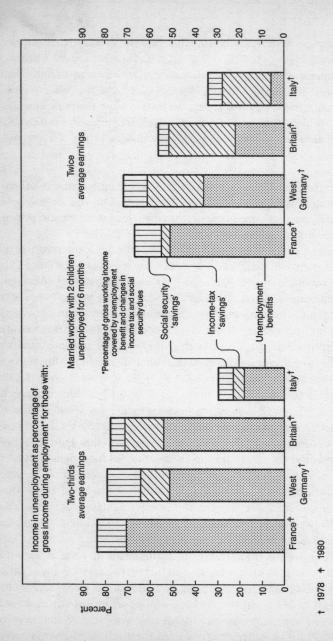

Figure 7 Replacement ratios compared. (Source: OECD, 1985.)

If the current replacement ratio in the UK still discourages active job-seeking, it is likely to do so among those on the register who would expect to receive earnings well below the national average if they were working. Between 1976 and 1980 a married man with two children on two-thirds of net average earnings when in work would have received 78 per cent of his earnings in Supplementary Benefit when unemployed. The results of a 1982 study by the DHSS of a cohort of 2,000 unemployed men are, therefore, particularly relevant, especially as their earnings when in work were well below the national average. First, for almost half the sample, unemployment benefits replaced *less than half* of their net earnings; only 6 per cent were better off unemployed. Using the broader definition of 'family income replacement ratio' (i.e. including types of income other than the man's net earnings), a third of the sample had incomes out of work which were less than half those in work, a quarter had incomes out of work at least 80 per cent of their incomes in work, and 9 per cent were marginally better off unemployed. Those who had the lowest 'family income replacement ratios' were predominantly young with few or no dependants and when in work were comparatively well paid. Those men with the highest replacement ratios were generally middle-aged with dependent children; if they were married their wives were less likely to be working; they were more likely to be in receipt of Supplementary Benefit and in their last jobs were likely to have earnings well below the average. One important reason for the high replacement ratios of men in this category was their very low take-up of means-tested benefits while they were in work.[9] It must be emphasized, however, that only about a quarter of those who are currently receiving either UB or SB have *any* dependants for whom they can claim benefit. The weekly income of £30 or less which claimants with no dependants may expect to receive can hardly be regarded as a serious 'disincentive' to seek work.

The results of this research do not differ greatly from those reported by Daniel in the early 1970s insofar as they confirm the essential characteristics – low income in work, middle age, relatively numerous dependants – of those men who are likely to be better off unemployed than working. We must, however, note the possibility that the quarter of the DHSS cohort who had replacement ratios of at least 80 per cent would choose to stay unemployed in preference to the physical and mental strain, plus the additional financial costs, of working.[10] Are these the 'sturdy beggars', the welfare parasites for whom life should be made less comfortable so that their incentive to work will be sharpened? If so, then there must be some evidence that relatively high benefit payments are inducing men who would otherwise be quite capable of obtaining work to remain unemployed. Daniel found no general indication that this was the case: 'The overwhelming weight of evidence pointed to the conclusion that it was the physical, social and psychological characteristics of workers: their age, stage in the life cycle, number of dependants, strength, state of health, and level in society when working, that determined how keen they were to work and that the level of benefits played a very small part in the overall picture.'[11] Only where a worker was already 'marginal' for any of these reasons, which meant in turn that his *prospects* for getting work were poor, was the level of benefit received likely to cool his interest in getting another job. A subsequent survey by Political and Economic Planning (PEP) underlined the relationship between the number of dependants, especially children, the marginal characteristics of the worker and the size of his 'asking price' for a job: '. . . the more children men had, the more they tended to be unfit and low-skilled. Child dependency allowances led men to seek higher levels of pay and consequently to be out of work longer.'[12] The DHSS cohort study confirms that men with four or more dependent children are likely to encounter great difficulties getting off the register.[13]

In general, however, there is no evidence to suggest that any more than a small minority of the unemployed are unconcerned about getting another job. Only about one-fifth of Daniel's sample either said they had no intention of finding a job or attached little importance to doing so, but this minority 'were by no means voluntarily unemployed in the sense of being fit and able to find jobs but preferring not to work'.[14] They were, on the contrary, composed of older workers nearing retirement, the sick, the disabled and women who intended to withdraw from the labour force. The rest of the sample were not only keen to get work but were very open-minded in their approach to job-seeking. Their flexibility was reflected in the fact that roughly one-third took new jobs which were at a lower grade of skill or status than their previous jobs had been and most, especially the older workers, accepted jobs which paid less in real terms. Only a small minority who were better off on benefit or had high wage expectations turned down a significant number of jobs. The authors of the DHSS study have arrived at broadly similar conclusions. The flexibility of the majority of the cohort is again emphasized by the fact that of those who found new jobs, three-quarters changed either the industry in which they were employed or their occupation, and more moved to a lower than to a higher level of skill. In terms of earnings, relatively few managed to improve their pay and at least one-third took jobs in which their real earnings were reduced. The level of interest in getting work was, and remained, high except among men over fifty, where ill health and early retirement discouraged job-seeking activity.[15]

Before concluding this section we must touch briefly on two further arguments which are occasionally advanced in support of the proposition that the financial 'shock absorber' is strong enough to discourage many of the unemployed from seeking jobs. First, it is claimed that redundancy payments often cushion the entry into unemployment and, by implication, delay the search for new employment. In reality, however, only a small minority of workers who register as unemployed in a given year are likely to have received any redundancy payments and in very few cases are these likely to exceed £2,000. Second, it is argued that a substantial number of those who are unemployed, and receiving benefit, have jobs in the black economy – informal, part-time employment which is rewarded in cash or in kind. It is certainly possible that some of the 200,000 'economically inactive' benefit claimants who were, at the time of the 1984 Labour Force Survey, found to be in employment would fall into this category. By definition, however, there is no means of assessing either the significance of the black economy or the extent to which the unemployed participate in it. Again, it would be surprising if more than a small minority of the total number of unemployed, whether registered or unregistered, derive a regular income from this form of economic activity. It should also be remembered that a large proportion of 'moonlighting' is almost certainly done by people who already have either part-time or full-time jobs.

To summarize, the 'equilibrium' analysis of unemployment to which reference was made at the start of this section seems to bear little relationship to the reality of the problem in Britain at the present time. It may, of course, be correct to say that *some* of the rise in unemployment up to the mid-1970s reflected a growth in frictional unemployment as 'fussy' voluntary quitters stayed on the register rather longer than they might have done had the benefit/earnings ratio been lower, although Daniel's work in the early 1970s does not support this hypothesis.[16] Any suggestion, however, that the growth in the stock of unemployment since 1973 has been caused primarily by a rise in the level of benefit-supported voluntary unemployment must be rejected. In the downswings of 1974–6 and 1979–82 the sharp rise in the un-employed stock was the result of a fall in employment op-portunities, so that many of those who were either 'shaken out' of employment by mass redundancies or 'shut out' by restrictions on recruitment were obliged to spend longer on the register. In such circumstances most employees tend to hang on to their jobs and labour turnover rates decline. Those who wish to change their jobs are most unlikely to go to the lengths of be-coming unemployed simply in order to pursue a full-time job search.

The increasing duration of completed unemployment spells and the growing proportion of the unemployed stock who remain on the register for more than six months cannot be attributed to a significant improvement in the benefit/earnings ratio, since no such improvement has occurred. On the contrary, the living standards of the majority of those who find themselves out of work for more than six months have almost certainly fallen since 1979. Indeed, it has been part of the present government's strategy that the real value of unemployment benefit should be reduced. There is no evidence that the majority of the un-employed, whether short-term or long-term, entertain un-realistically high expectations or that they frequently turn down job offers. However choosy some of the unemployed may have been in the days when total unemployment was less than 3 per cent, the evidence suggests that there is now considerable flexibility in their attitude to whatever jobs are available. There is no evidence that before the start of the current recession in 1979 the proportion of the unemployed who were better off out of work than in work exceeded 10 per cent of the total, and this proportion has almost certainly diminished since then. A reduction in the level of benefit paid to members of this minority, whatever symbolic value it may have, is unlikely to drive them back to work since they tend to exhibit several characteristics which place them in the most marginal segment of the labour market. If it is indeed the case that most of those who stay on the register for more than six months do so not from choice but from necessity, there seems little point in punishing them for something which is not their fault.

## SUMMARY

Supply-side factors throw much valuable light on the growth of unemployment in the UK over the past decade or so, but they do not explain most of it. A growing population of working age does not inevitably lead to a rise in unemployment. Much depends on the activity rates of the various groups within the working-age population which are, in turn, strongly influenced by the relevant employment opportunities, or in other words by the demand for labour. Between 1977 and 1983 falling male and female activity rates reduced the unemployment effects of a rising working-age population. Conversely, in 1983–4 a sharp rise in the female activity combined with an upturn in the population effect to increase unemployment, despite a rise in employment opportunities. The tendency during the recent cyclical upswing for employment and unemployment to rise together, the phenomenon of 'jobless growth', is attributable to the growth of part-time jobs. Part-time employment strongly favours women, while the number of full-time jobs for both men and women continues to decline. Projected rates of growth in both the working-age population and the female activity rate are likely to

keep registered unemployment at high levels for the rest of the
decade, unless, of course, the economy can improve its rate of
job-creation. The growth in the British labour force has not been
faster than that of other advanced industrial economies – indeed,
the rise in the working-age population has been relatively
modest. Nor do trends in working hours help to explain Britain's
current problem since average hours worked are now significantly lower than in certain other countries where unemployment is also lower.

The argument that a large proportion of current unemployment
is voluntary in character due to an allegedly high level of benefits
must also be rejected. All the evidence suggests that most of
those who are on the unemployment register are there not from
choice but necessity, and for them the experience of unemployment is financially far from comfortable. Only a small
minority of the unemployed are likely to be discouraged from
seeking work by relatively high ratios of benefit to potential
earnings and these are in any case likely to be among the most
marginal participants in the labour market.

Consequently we must look to the demand side of the labour
market for the most important causes of the growth in unemployment.

# CHAPTER 3

# THE LABOUR MARKET: DEMAND

*Inflation is not an alternative to unemployment but one of its principal causes. Today's unemployment was not created by this Government but is the result of years of overmanning and restrictive practices, madcap strikes for higher pay for less work, and attacks on profits, destroying the resources to invest in new jobs ... Today's unemployment is the price we are having to pay for putting off for far too long the fight against inflation.*

Sir Geoffrey Howe, Chancellor of the Exchequer, 1982

*We cannot hope to raise our productivity fast enough to balance our overseas accounts and increase our rate of growth if the share of resources devoted to manufacturing continues to fall.*

Denis Healey, Chancellor of the Exchequer, 1975

The main proximate cause of the rise in unemployment in Britain since the 1970s has been the decline in total employment relative to the growth of the working population. Some economists maintain that this combination of rising unemployment and a growing supply of labour should not exist at all. In a world of freely competitive markets in which all prices are flexible, an over-supply of any commodity must lead to a fall in its price relative to that of substitutes, thereby stimulating demand and clearing the market for that commodity. If, therefore, the supply of labour exceeds demand, a fall in its price relative to the cost of capital must occur. This implies a fall in real wages or, more accurately, in the real supply cost of labour to employers. Workers will then price themselves back into jobs as employers stop substituting capital (i.e. machinery) for labour and unemployment will fall. The fact that workers are not, apparently, pricing themselves back into the labour market – particularly in Western Europe – is commonly attributed to the excessive power of trade unions, the misguided pay policies of employers and the tardiness of governments in cutting taxes on employment such as national insurance contributions. The implications for policy, however, are clear – if we can make the labour market work properly, unemployment will fall.

This approach, however, begs several questions. If real wages do indeed determine the level of employment, what factors influence real wages? Is it not the case that in an advanced industrial society there are many labour markets and that they work at different levels of efficiency? If, for example, the real wages of a particular type of labour are rising, might this not be the result of growing *demand* for it? Between 1979 and 1983, for example, most non-manual occupations in the British economy saw both an expansion of employment opportunities *and* a rise in their real earnings. Manual occupations, by contrast, despite the supposed advantage of relatively strong trade union organization, experienced both a substantial decline in employment *and* a slight fall in real earnings. In other words, the fact that some sectors of employment are expanding and some are contracting does not seem to be directly attributable to changes in their real earnings. Our attention should therefore be focused on the structural changes in the demand for labour which have occurred not only in the UK but in most other advanced industrial economies over the past two decades or so and on the relationship between these changes and the growth of unemployment.


## HAVE WORKERS PRICED THEMSELVES OUT OF JOBS?

Whether real wages in the UK are 'too high' or not, the first point to recognize is that they are not primarily determined in the labour market. Employers and trade unions periodically fix increases in money wages, but the *real* wage enjoyed by the employees covered by the hundreds of collective agreements negotiated in the UK every year is determined by a range of economic variables which are outside the control of the parties to these agreements. These variables include the exchange rate, the level of foreign competition and, of course, the government's own fiscal and monetary policies. Since these variables affect the price competitiveness of British industry in both home and export markets, they also influence the level of employment and un-employment. As such they will be discussed later in this chapter.

The factors which influence the collective negotiation of money wages in the private sector include the employer's ability to pay, the past and anticipated rise in the cost of living and the current level of increases being negotiated by other comparable groups. Obviously the relative importance of these factors tends to vary with the general level of economic activity and with the par-ticular circumstances of the bargainers themselves.

It might be supposed that the experience of the recession, with unprecedented levels of bankruptcies and redundancies, would have concentrated the minds of wage bargainers exclusively on the ability of the enterprise to sustain increases in its total pay bill. The application of this criterion should in turn have resulted in a much closer link between earnings and productivity. There is some evidence that during the depths of the recession in 1981–2 this is more or less what happened. During the subsequent upswing, however, earnings growth revived quite strongly and moved ahead of productivity. Managerial arguments for low or zero pay increases which carry conviction at a time when the enterprise is facing very depressed demand conditions and widespread job losses are occurring tend to lose their force when output and profits are recovering and stability of employment is returning. Moreover, the conspicuous reluctance of manufac-turing companies to recruit additional labour to increase output implies considerable reliance on both overtime and output-related incentive schemes. Between 1981 and 1984 the volume of overtime working rose from 9·3 million to 11·6 million hours, which virtually restored it to pre-recession levels. From 1982 onwards average earnings growth in manufacturing exceeded basic wage rates by 3 to 4 per cent a year.

Other criteria which are influential during 'normal' economic conditions include the cost of living and comparability. During the 1970s, when inflation was relatively rapid and unpredictable, it was usually easy for trade union negotiators to demonstrate that since the last annual pay settlement their members' earnings had been seriously eroded in real terms by the rising cost of living. Managements have tended to be sympathetic to this argument and, although temporarily set aside in some cases during the exceptional conditions of 1981–2, it has subsequently re-established itself as a major influence in pay bargaining. The continued existence of an annual wage round and a going rate for settlements in an era of relatively low and stable inflation underlines the significance of this appeal to 'fairness' and social equity. The fact that a worker's earnings keep pace with or even exceed the cost of living, however, will not in itself ensure that he is satisfied with his pay. Bargaining over pay typically takes place within a well-established framework of comparative reference points. Indeed, most pay agreements are ultimately bargains about *differentials* and *relativities*, which in turn express both social and market-related needs. Trade union negotiators typically emphasize the fairness of maintaining recognized pay relationships both within and between bargaining units. Management also has a direct interest in differentials and relativities insofar as they influence the ability of the enterprise to attract and retain key groups of workers and improve employee morale and productivity. The principles which dominate the process of wage bargaining – and which are influential even in non-union enterprises – make it very unlikely, therefore, that employers will insist on reducing the real earnings of their existing employees merely in order to finance the marginal creation of new jobs.

Beveridge repeatedly warned that full employment would be endangered if employers and trade unionists did not behave with moderation and restraint and to this end he advocated the general adoption of quasi-compulsory arbitration procedures. In the event, however, the postwar period merely witnessed the extension of an unreformed system of collective bargaining to cover a larger area of British industry and, in some industries, an increasing tendency for unionized workgroups to strike in pursuit of higher real wages. It is worth recalling that in 1960, after more than a decade of steady but by later standards very gentle inflation, Beveridge warned that 'If the organizations that now determine wages continue to demand and to give more money for less work, the people of Britain must choose between estab-

lishing some State control of prices and suffering endless inflation which will debase our currency ...'[1] In other words,
Beveridge (and indeed many other observers) believed that, in
conditions of full employment, inflation could arise not simply
from excessive demand but also from the tendency for wages to
grow faster than productivity. The obvious course of action was
for governments to intervene in 'free' collective bargaining by
one means or another in order to restrain the growth of money
wages, in addition to managing aggregate demand. Incomes
policy was therefore added to the existing weapons of fiscal and
monetary policy in the government's counter-inflationary
armoury.

Incomes policies have, however, at best achieved only transient
success – holding down pay settlements for two or three years,
only to be blown apart by subsequent 'explosions' as wage
bargainers make up the lost ground. Incomes policies have failed
partly because they have typically challenged one or more of the
established criteria for wage bargaining outlined above. Another
cause of failure, however, lies in the changing structure of collective bargaining in the UK.

In structural terms there has, over the past twenty years or so,
been a decisive shift in the focus of wage bargaining away from
industry-wide agreements towards plant and company level. Although national-level agreements still influence basic terms and
conditions in some manufacturing industries, notably engineering, a large and growing proportion of total earnings is
fixed by bargaining within individual companies and establishments. Another significant development is the tendency for large-
scale employers across industry as a whole to break away from
national agreements altogether and reshape their pay structures
and bargaining arrangements in the light of their own needs.[2]
The general impact of this progressive decentralization in the
framework of pay determination is to emphasize the priorities of
individual enterprises, which do not, of course, necessarily
coincide with the attempts of successive governments, through
the medium of incomes policy, to keep the overall growth of
earnings in line with productivity.

All incomes policies reflect a cost-push view of the inflationary process in which money wages and prices are propelled upwards by a mixture of social, psychological and institutional forces. On this view the level of employment is strongly influenced by the extent to which the upward push on costs can be controlled. An alternative diagnosis stresses the importance of excessive monetary demand – of too much expenditure chasing too little production. On this view inflation can only be reduced or eliminated if excess demand is also removed, which means that unemployment will rise. Support for this diagnosis was – and for some economists still is – provided by the Phillips Curve. Phillips examined the relationship between changes in money wage rates and the level of unemployment over the period 1861 to 1957 and found that low unemployment was associated with large increases in money wages and vice versa.[3] The implication for policy-makers was that governments could, by managing aggregate demand, trade inflation off against unemployment. The belief in a benign trade-off was no doubt confirmed by postwar experience. Between 1948 and 1966 retail prices increased by 3 to 4 per cent a year, average weekly earnings rose in *real* terms by 2·5 per cent a year and unemployment was on average less than 2 per cent. Indeed, up to the late 1960s it was generally believed that if unemployment was allowed to rise to 2·5 per cent, inflation could be eliminated completely.[4] Towards the end of the 1960s, however, inflation and unemployment started to rise together and during the 1970s the Phillips Curve moved further and further outwards, implying higher rates of inflation at any given level of unemployment. When, then, did this benign combination of low inflation and low unemployment disappear? One answer, broadly identified with Friedmanite monetarism, relies on the notion that there is a *natural* rate of unemployment at which the rate of inflation is constant.[5] If governments seek to reduce unemployment below its natural rate by misguided policies of monetary expansion, inflation will simply accelerate and unemployment will sooner or later return to the natural rate. At the natural rate, the supply of labour is in equilibrium with demand, or in other words the *real* wage rate is at a level which will induce employers to take on more labour. When real wages are at their market-clearing level, *involuntary* un-

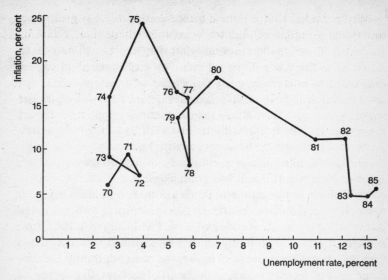

Figure 8   Inflation and unemployment in the United Kingdom, 1970–
85. (Source: *Employment Gazette*, various issues.)

employment cannot exist. If workers are still unemployed the
reason must lie in their wrong-headed determination to hold out
for a higher real wage than they can actually get.

What, then, determines the natural rate and what does it mean
in terms of the number of people out of work? Monetarists hold
that the natural rate is produced by a combination of 'real'
factors in the labour market such as the characteristics of the
labour force (age, skill, geographical distribution), the nature and
distribution of vacancies, and the existence of trade union
monopolies and other structural immobilities. Should any of
these barriers to the free play of market forces become more
formidable – for example, as a result of government incomes
policies or pro-trade union legislation – the natural rate of
unemployment will increase. By the same token a policy of expanding aggregate demand will simply produce more inflation:
the natural rate of unemployment can be reduced only by improving the working of the labour market. Many monetarists
would accept, however, that there is a short-run trade-off between inflation and unemployment and that the Phillips Curve

'works' provided that a price expectations variable is grafted on to it. Since employers and trade unionists base their decisions about money wage increases on what they expect will happen to prices over the life of their agreements, expectations of higher inflation will effectively push the Phillips Curve outwards. But once inflation is fully anticipated, the actual rate will equal the expected rate and the natural rate of unemployment will reassert itself. The Phillips Curve is then vertical, inflation is fully anticipated and there is no *involuntary* unemployment.

A major weakness in the 'natural rate' hypothesis, however, at least from a policy-maker's point of view, is that it is notoriously difficult to quantify and predict. Monetarists may say with conviction that since the early 1970s the natural rate has risen, but where it currently stands and how it will behave in the future remain unclear.[6] It certainly cannot be assumed that the rate is impervious to the pressure of aggregate demand, if only because some of the factors which influence it (such as the degree of 'mismatch' between unemployed and vacancies, the readiness of workers to change their jobs and the level of labour productivity) are themselves influenced by the level of economic activity. By the same token it cannot be assumed that there is a direct, one-dimensional link between real wages and the level of employment which dictates that the former must be reduced if the latter is to be increased. In an economy where there is a large margin of unused resources and where even relatively efficient firms are operating below capacity (as in the UK at the time of writing), an increase in activity will tend to reduce the real unit cost of labour and increase profits. If, in the ensuing upswing, productivity continues to rise, one can envisage a situation in which falling unemployment is not incompatible with higher real wages. As Thirlwall has pointed out, the payment of wages is both a cost to employers and a major component of aggregate demand.[7] If real wage *costs* can be reduced either by cuts in employers' overhead charges on labour or by advances in productivity while real wage *levels* are kept stable, it should be possible to combine a fall in the level of unemployment with reasonably stable inflation. A *cut* in workers' real earnings, however, particularly if this was substantial and lasted over a period of years, would not only reduce demand but would eventually provoke a wage explosion as the more powerful, well-organized workgroups sought to recover the lost ground.

This brings us back to the 'cost-push' view of inflation, or at least to that version of it which stresses the importance of real wage targets in the process of pay determination. The motor of both inflation and unemployment is said to be the determination of increasingly powerful workgroups and trade unions to assert their 'right' to higher standards of living, even at the cost of putting less well-organized fellow workers out of a job. As such, this view puts more emphasis on social and institutional factors than on market forces and, in particular, suggests that a sea-change occurred in workers' attitudes during the second half of the 1960s. In Bispham's words:

The fact that the Phillips Curve 'worked' up to 1966–7 can be explained by allowing that the trade unions cooperated with the full employment policy by, in effect, restraining the new power which full employment gave them. What is more, the strength of this restraint increased if unemployment rose a little as memories of the pre-war experience were revived and vice versa. Gradually, as these memories faded, and as a new generation reached prime working age, this restraint was relaxed, and thus the rate of wage increase demanded rose sharply.[8]

This 'new militancy' was not, of course, peculiar to Britain; most other industrialized market economies experienced stronger wage-push inflation during the 1970s than in the previous decade. The gap between the expectations of organized labour and the level of real incomes which the economy could sustain, however, was undoubtedly wider in Britain than elsewhere. This was not so much due to exceptional stupidity on the part of British union officials, although the growing influence of the extreme left within certain unions was hardly conducive to greater moderation in wage bargaining, as to the constraints imposed by a low-productivity economy.[9] Between 1970 and 1980 average earnings in the UK rose by 341 per cent whereas output per employee crept up by a mere 27 per cent. By contrast, Britain's major competitors increased their average earnings by about half the British rate (190 per cent) but enjoyed roughly twice the increase in productivity (51 per cent). The strength of union wage-push in Britain since the late 1960s may therefore be seen as a reaction to slowly rising standards of living and thus, ultimately, to slowly rising productivity, even if union-inspired restrictive working practices have themselves helped to retard productivity growth.

The continuing force of wage-push in the British economy does not, however, mean that there is now *no* trade-off between inflation and unemployment. During the extraordinarily sharp recession of 1980–82, managements' much-reduced ability to meet inflationary wage claims – particularly in the manufacturing sector – exerted a much stronger influence over the process of pay determination than in the 1970s and the level of settlements fell precipitately, in some cases below the general rate of inflation. The fact that the Phillips Curve appears to have 'worked' during this period, therefore, was due not so much to the presence of a growing 'reserve army' of unemployed outside the factory gates, bidding down the going rate of pay settlements, as to the desire of employers to avoid bankruptcy and the fear of unemployment among their employees. A reinterpretation of the Phillips Curve suggests that the rate of growth of money wages depends on the *rate of change* as well as the level of unemployment. A rapid rise in unemployment, sustained over two or three bargaining rounds, is indeed likely to affect pay settlements but once unemployment levels off, its influence on bargaining seems to decline quite quickly. The Phillips Curve, as can be seen from Figure 8 above, is more accurately a loop. It follows that there is little prospect of *permanently* reducing wage inflation by relying on the continuing existence of high unemployment. Nor is there any realistic prospect of a reduction in unemployment through a generally lower level of real wages.


## THE CHANGING STRUCTURE OF EMPLOYMENT

A conspicuous feature of the British, and indeed of most other advanced economies in recent years, is the declining importance of the industrial sector, both as a source of employment and as a contributor to GDP. In terms of employment the decline has been both relative and absolute. At the start of the 1970s roughly 46 per cent of employees in employment worked in the industrial sector (i.e. in manufacturing, construction and energy). By the end of the decade, however, this share had fallen to barely 40 per cent and during the first half of the 1980s the rate of decline accelerated, so that by the end of 1985 only 33 per cent of all employees worked in the industrial sector. A falling industrial share does not *necessarily* lead to higher total unemployment, even in the context of an increase in the population of working age. Much depends on the rate at which *non-industrial* employment is growing and the extent to which this type of employment offers a substitute for jobs in the industrial sector. The broad structural changes in Britain's employment base are summarized in Table 3.

It is evident from this table that between 1971 and 1979 a loss of nearly one million industrial jobs was more than offset by the growth in service sector employment and the total number of employees in employment rose by one million. Yet over the same period *unemployment* also rose from 700,000 to over 1·3 million, implying a significant mismatch between the characteristics of job-seekers and the requirements of the jobs available in the expanding sectors. This mismatch became more pronounced between 1979 and 1985, when the industrial sector contracted by nearly a quarter. The service sector as a whole grew only marginally over this period and, as we noted above (p. 32), virtually all the new jobs created were for part-time females. It is hardly surprising, therefore, that Britain should now have a major problem of long-term unemployment among male manual workers.

This absolute as well as relative decline in industrial employment is viewed by many observers not only as the major cause of high unemployment but as symptomatic of deep-seated weaknesses in the British economy and of an equally fundamental social hostility to wealth-creation. This view was articulated towards the end of 1985 by the House of Lords Select Committee on Overseas Trade and is shared by many British industrialists. Before considering this analysis in more detail,

**Table 3    The changing structure of employment, 1971–85**

| | Employees (millions) | | | | % Change | | |
|---|---|---|---|---|---|---|---|
| | 1971 | 1974 | 1979 | 1985 | 1971–9 | 1979–85 | 1971–85 |
| Production and construction industries | 9·9 | 9·7 | 9·0 | 6·9 | −8·5 | −23·7 | −30·1 |
| Manufacturing | 7·9 | 7·7 | 7·1 | 5·3 | −10·2 | −24·5 | −32·1 |
| All services | 11·3 | 12·2 | 13·2 | 13·5 | +16·5 | +2·6 | +20·0 |
| Wholesale distribution | 0·9 | 1·0 | 1·1 | 1·1 | +14·3 | +6·7 | +22·0 |
| Retail distribution | 1·9 | 2·0 | 2·1 | 2·1 | +9·3 | +0·9 | +10·3 |
| Hotels and catering | 0·7 | 0·8 | 0·9 | 1·0 | +35·6 | +11·0 | +50·6 |
| Transport | 1·1 | 1·0 | 1·0 | 0·8 | −4·5 | −18·6 | −22·3 |
| Telecommunications | 0·4 | 0·4 | 0·4 | 0·4 | −5·0 | +1·4 | −3·6 |
| Banking, insurance and finance | 1·3 | 1·4 | 1·6 | 1·9 | +24·6 | +19·0 | +46·6 |
| Public administration | 1·7 | 1·8 | 1·9 | 1·8 | +12·6 | −7·6 | +4·7 |
| Education | 1·2 | 1·4 | 1·6 | 1·5 | +26·2 | −3·4 | +22·0 |
| Health services | 0·9 | 1·0 | 1·2 | 1·3 | +26·3 | +10·9 | +40·0 |
| Other services | 0·9 | 1·0 | 1·2 | 1·3 | +29·1 | +8·5 | +40·0 |
| All industries and services | 21·6 | 22·3 | 22·6 | 20·8 | +4·5 | −8·0 | −3·8 |

(Source: *Employment Gazette*, various issues.)

however, we should remember that neither a relative nor even an absolute decline in industrial employment *necessarily* gives cause for concern. Firstly, the same trend is to a greater or less extent apparent in most other mature industrialized market economies.

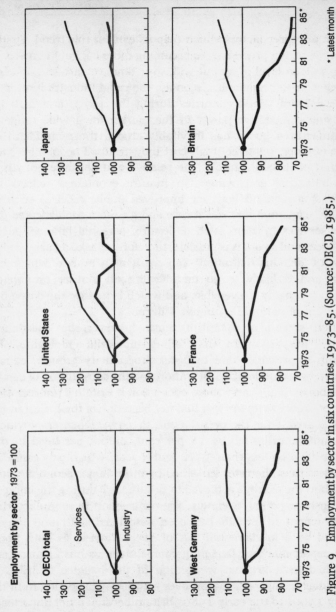

Figure 9   Employment by sector in six countries, 1973–85. (Source: OECD, 1985.)

There are three factors which help us explain this trend. Firstly, manufacturing processes are becoming more capital intensive, so that a given level of output will, over time, require less and less manpower to produce it. Secondly, the rapid industrialization of several Third World countries during the 1970s and their increasing competitive power in the market for a wide range of manufactured goods has inevitably eroded the manufacturing base of older, relatively high-cost industrialized economies such as that of Britain. Thirdly, the relative and absolute growth of non-industrial employment in mature economies reflects an increasing demand both for improved public services such as health, education and social care and for more sophisticated private services in areas such as leisure, personal finance, entertainment and so on. It is possible, therefore, to take a fairly benign view of 'deindustrialization' and see it as a process which has been and is likely to go on affecting all mature economies, which is broadly irreversible, and which is neither the cause nor the effect of national economic failure.

Such superficial optimism must, however, be questioned. Firstly, the argument that falling industrial employment in Britain is primarily due to faster productivity growth, caused in turn by technological innovation and the substitution of capital for labour, might carry more conviction if Britain's pre-recession rate of productivity growth had not been one of the lowest in the OECD area. Over the period 1966 to 1979, when employment in manufacturing fell by 16 per cent, output per head in this sector grew by less than 3 per cent a year, which was considerably less than the rates sustained by other major economies and less than the average achieved in Britain itself during the immediate postwar period. Secondly, the contraction in manufacturing employment in Britain has been associated with and largely caused by a fundamental loss of *competitiveness* in both home and export markets. Declining competitiveness has in turn been reflected in a gradual weakening of the balance of trade in manufactured goods, so that over a twenty-year period from the early 1960s to the early 1980s Britain became a net importer of these goods (Figure 10).

The growing tendency over this period for increases in domestic consumer spending to suck in progressively greater volumes

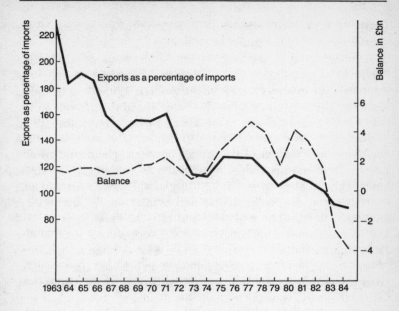

Figure 10    Balance of trade in manufactured goods, 1963–84. (Source: *Monthly Review of External Trade Statistics*, April 1985.)

of foreign manufactured goods while British companies were operating well below capacity cannot simply be shrugged off as the inevitable consequences of industrialization elsewhere. Britain's failure to compete was and still is most conspicuous in relation to other mature economies such as West Germany and Japan. This lack of competitiveness is apparent not only in 'mature product' industries such as motor vehicles, where the UK sustained a trading deficit of £2·7 billion in 1985, but also in the so-called 'sunrise' sectors of information technology and electronics, which recorded a deficit of £2 billion in 1984.[10] Against the relatively advanced economies of the EEC, Britain's deficit on manufactured trade rose from £639 million in 1977 to £8 billion in 1983. A similar trend is apparent in trade with other OECD members outside the EEC, where the deficit rose from £166 million in 1977 to nearly £5 billion in 1983. The only countries with which Britain is still in surplus on its manufactured trade are Middle Eastern oil-producers and some former colonial territories, none of which provides a particularly healthy basis for the future.

This declining performance against other advanced economies helps us to put the structural shift in favour of non-industrial employment in a more realistic perspective. While it is true that certain other countries have also experienced this change in the distribution of employment, it seems to have been sharper in Britain than elsewhere (Figure 9). Those who still cling to a benign interpretation of this trend, however, claim that as one of the most mature industrial societies in the world, Britain is inevitably in the vanguard of the general movement towards service-based or 'post-industrial' economies. In Britain services now account for about 50 per cent of GDP by volume and 65 per cent of total employment – lower proportions than in the USA but significantly greater than in West Germany, Japan and Italy. But while the presumed relationship between high levels of real disposable income and the growth of services justifies the very large service sector in the USA, it is by no means clear that the current commitment to services in the UK truly reflects the real wealth of the British economy. It certainly seems strange that the service sector should be proportionately greater in the UK than in West Germany and Japan, despite their much higher levels of per capita GDP. It should also be noted (Figure 9) that since the mid-1970s both the USA and Japan have increased *both* their industrial and their service employment, which suggests that growth in the latter need not be associated with, let alone cause, a decline in the former.

A more relaxed view of the shift out of industrial employment in Britain might be justified *if* British consumers were losing their taste for imported manufacturing goods and *if* the vitality of the service sector was not directly dependent on the competitive strength of the industrial sector, particularly of those industries which contribute heavily to the balance of payments. In an economy, however, which is more dependent on world trade than most of its competitors and in which manufactured goods still contribute roughly half of total export earnings, the performance of the industrial sector as a whole has a major effect on the general rate of economic growth and, therefore, on standards of living. Since the employment-creating capacity of the service sector, whether publicly or privately owned, depends heavily on the level of real disposable income, the prospects for reducing the overall level of *unemployment* are heavily influenced by the competitiveness of manufacturing industry.

The increasingly adverse balance of trade in manufactured goods suggests that the growth of unemployment in Britain is due not so much to any serious deficiency in aggregate demand as to a progressive failure on the supply side of the economy. Over the past two decades aggregate demand has been strong enough to sustain higher levels of domestic output and employment than have in fact been achieved. The fact that during the recession of 1980–82 both industrial employment and output fell much more sharply in Britain than elsewhere while the appetite of British consumers for foreign goods continued to increase clearly points to serious deficiencies on the supply side. What, then, are these deficiencies and why have they arisen?

## THE PROBLEM OF COMPETITIVENESS

Analyses of industrial competitiveness conventionally distinguish between price and non-price factors. It is often argued that British industry has 'priced itself out of world markets' by failing to control its costs, just as British workers are said to have 'priced themselves out of a job' by insisting on excessive wage settlements. This, of course, greatly oversimplifies the problem. A major and sustained depreciation in the exchange value of sterling would not *in itself* be enough to reverse the long decline in Britain's share of world trade in manufactured goods, any more than a general reduction in real wages would reduce unemployment.

Successive commentators, going back over a century, have repeatedly drawn attention to a wide range of non-price factors as the dominant influence on British industrial performance.[11] Although much of this evidence is subjective and qualitative in character, it is too frequently encountered to be dismissed. It clearly points to serious competitive deficiencies in areas such as product quality, design features, marketing skill, manufacturing efficiency, after-sales service and general organizational ability which compare badly with the standards normally attained by American, German and, more recently, Japanese rivals. Non-price factors cannot, however, be regarded as wholly separate from price and cost competitiveness since both involve the application of managerial skill.

It is generally agreed that the best measure of international price competitiveness is relative unit labour costs. A reduction in unit costs relative to those of competitors allows either an improvement in price competitiveness (possibly leading to an increase in demand) or an increase in profit margins (possibly resulting in higher investment and output). This yardstick in turn combines three other factors – relative labour costs or earnings levels, labour productivity and the exchange rate. Roughly 70 per cent of final costs in manufacturing industry are made up of employment costs, the bulk of which reflect the level of earnings. In Britain the proportion attributable to earnings is significantly higher than in most other EEC countries, which makes British industry's poor performance in controlling wage inflation even more serious than it might otherwise be. As we noted earlier in this chapter, since the late 1960s money wages in the UK have been tending to rise faster than in other major competitor countries with particularly large increases in the mid and late 1970s. Between 1980 and 1983 Britain's performance improved relative to that of France and Italy but not to that of West Germany, Japan and the USA. Since 1983, however, wage inflation in the UK has regained its traditional momentum and in 1985 earnings growth in manufacturing averaged about 9 per cent, more than double that of West Germany and Japan.

The second major determinant of cost competitiveness is productivity. Researchers have found a strong association between success in export markets and the rapidity of productivity growth. A survey of British manufacturing as a whole over the period 1950–73 found that those industries whose productivity increased relatively quickly were able to remain competitive, which in turn helped them raise their output and maintain their employment base. By the same token it was found that industries with the slowest productivity growth had suffered

the largest increases in import penetration.[12] The *average* performance of British industry, however, has been consistently poor
relative to that of most of its competitors. Up to 1974 average
annual productivity growth in British industry was, at least by
its own historical standards, quite high. Output per person
employed in manufacturing grew at an annual average of 2·4
per cent in 1955–60, rising to 4·4 per cent in 1963–8, and then
falling back slightly to 3·9 per cent in 1968–73. Britain's problem was that other leading industrial countries were doing
consistently better. It has been estimated that in 1955 labour
productivity in the UK was significantly higher than in West
Germany, France or Italy, yet by 1974 both France and West
Germany had gained a 30 per cent advantage. Between 1974
and 1980 productivity growth rates slowed down everywhere
but, at a mere 0·9 per cent a year, the average increase achieved
by British industry was exceptionally low, implying the widespread retention of under-employed labour. As a result the
productivity gap between Britain and its major competitors has
continued to widen (see Figure 11).

The exceptional rise of about 12 per cent in British manufacturing productivity which occurred in 1980–82, and which essentially reflected the fact that employment fell faster than output
during the recession, has made little or no difference to the gap
which separates Britain from its major competitors. A quantum
leap of about 40 per cent is still needed in order to bring British
manufacturing productivity levels into line with its major
partners in the EEC, and an even greater step change is required
to match American or Japanese levels.

Combining labour costs with productivity gives us the
yardstick of unit labour costs expressed in domestic currency and,
not surprisingly, Britain compares unfavourably with every
major competitor except Italy. Figure 12 also confirms that since
1983 British industry's competitiveness has once again begun to
deteriorate relative to that of West Germany, Japan and the
United States.

The third important influence on competitiveness is the exchange rate insofar as it translates national domestic costs into
internationally comparable terms. From 1970 to 1978 the
effective exchange rate of sterling against a basket of currencies

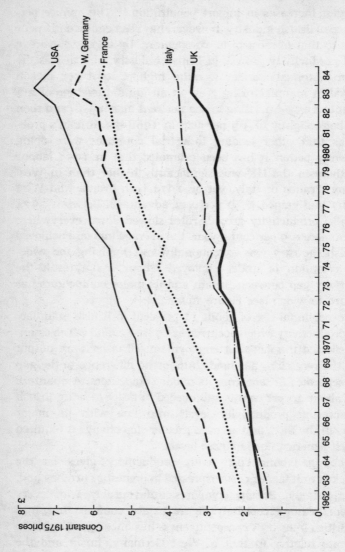

Figure 11  Productivity: manufacturing output per man hour* in UK £. (Sources: OECD, 1985.)

* Gross value added per man hour.

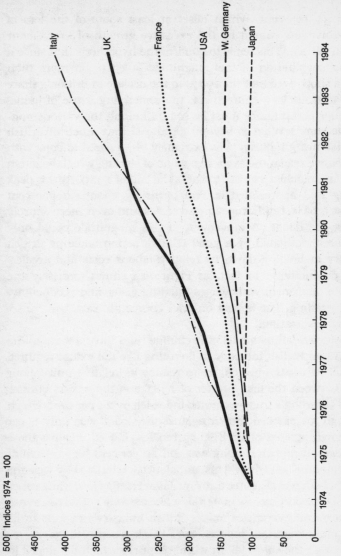

Figure 12  Unit labour cost: labour costs per unit of output in manufacturing in local currency. (Source: OECD, 1985.)

fell by 36 per cent, which offset at least some of the loss of competitiveness caused by the excessive growth of unit labour costs in Britain. This tends to confirm the hypothesis that since a sterling devaluation of this magnitude failed to do more than bring a short-lived halt (in 1977) to the decline in Britain's share of world trade in manufactures, the underlying cause of industry's poor performance must be sought among the various non-price factors.[13] What is beyond dispute is that much of British manufacturing industry was extremely ill-prepared to cope with the massive rise in the exchange value of sterling which began in 1978 and reached its peak towards the end of 1980. At this peak sterling had appreciated in real terms by about 50 per cent against a basket of European currencies and even more sharply against the dollar. A movement of this magnitude could only have been mitigated by a good relative performance by British industry in holding down its relative labour costs and accelerating productivity. In fact, as Figure 13 shows, precisely the opposite happened, with wages inflating faster and productivity actually falling. The impact on price competitiveness was consequently devastating.

Subsequent adjustments in exchange rates have not eased the pressure on British industry to anything like the extent required to offset its continuing failure to reduce its relative unit labour costs. Between the first quarter of 1981 and the second quarter of 1985 sterling's trade-weighted index fell by 24 per cent, which although 50 per cent down against the dollar was only 6 per cent down against other EEC currencies. Indeed, against these European currencies sterling was still 20 per cent higher than at the beginning of 1979. This unbalanced relationship was the worst of both worlds, since a strong dollar relative to sterling raises the cost of importing raw materials while a strong pound relative to key European currencies makes British industry's exports to its single most important market, the EEC, less competitive.

Although the sharp fall in world oil prices which developed in late 1985 and early 1986 caused a further decline in the exchange value of sterling against most major currencies, it will be two or three years before the full effects of this devaluation – assuming that it is not subsequently reversed – work through to

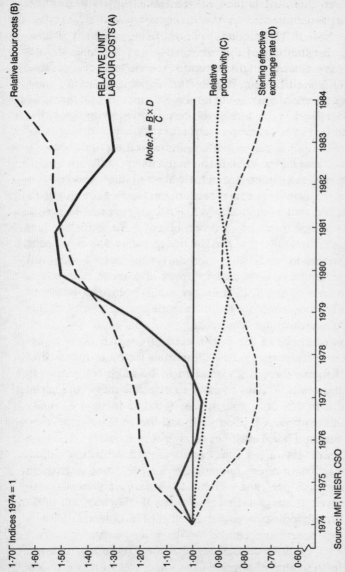

1·70  Indices 1974 = 1

1·60

1·50

1·40

1·30

1·20

1·10

1·00

0·90

0·80

0·70

0·60

1974  1975  1976  1977  1978  1979  1980  1981  1982  1983  1984

Relative labour costs (B)

RELATIVE UNIT
LABOUR COSTS (A)

Note: $A = \dfrac{B \times D}{C}$

Relative
productivity (C)

Sterling effective
exchange rate (D)

Source: IMF, NIESR, CSO

Figure 13  Sources of changes in UK competitiveness in manufacturing. (Relative unit labour costs, broken down into relative labour costs, relative productivity and the exchange rate.) (Source: House of Lords, Report from the Select Committee on Overseas Trade, HMSO, July 1985.)

exports. Even then, the impact will be limited unless significant improvements in non-price competitiveness are also achieved.

The shortfall in international competitiveness which British manufacturing industry as a whole still needs to overcome should make us wary of what might be termed the rhetoric of recovery. While it may well be true that individual companies are now much more aware of the need to improve their competitiveness in both price and non-price terms, the combination of high relative unit labour costs and an over-valued currency will, unless corrected, lead to further losses of market shares, output and jobs.

Whatever may be said about the inevitability of the decline of manufacturing in all advanced industrial economies, there is little doubt that in Britain the contraction has been exceptional in both its speed and magnitude. While all major manufacturing countries suffered from the recession of 1980–82, British industry was the first to suffer and the last to experience any significant recovery. Even in mid-1985 manufacturing output was still about 5 per cent less than its 1979 peak and about 10 per cent below the level of 1973. In no other major industrial economy has there been an absolute fall in manufacturing output of this magnitude and duration (Figure 14).

One characteristic of the British economy which helps to explain the severity of the decline in manufacturing output is that imports of manufactured goods seem to be more responsive to income changes in Britain than in most other major industrial countries. It has been estimated that Britain's income elasticity of demand for imports is about 1·6 and the world income elasticity of demand for British exports is about unity. Thus an annual rate of, say, 4 per cent output growth in Britain would, other things being equal, generate a 6·4 per cent growth in imports and a 4 per cent increase in exports. Thirlwall's estimates, however, suggest that there are no fewer than thirty manufacturing industries which have an income elasticity of demand for imports in excess of *two*. In other words, for every 1 per cent increase in real incomes in Britain there is a two-fold increase in the value of imported manufactures in this group of industries.[14] As a result, whenever domestic demand has shown significant growth, an increasing proportion of it has

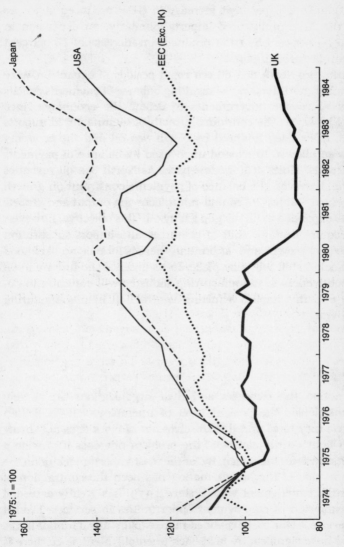

Figure 14 Manufacturing output, 1974–84. (Source: House of Lords, Report from the Select Committee on Overseas Trade, HMSO, July 1985.)

1975: 1 = 100

Japan

USA

EEC (Exc. UK)

UK

leaked out into imports. During the 'Barber boom' of 1972–3, for example, a 6 per cent increase in GDP produced a 30 per cent rise in manufactured imports. Similarly, an expansion in GDP of 3 per cent in 1983 produced an increase of 16 per cent in manufactured imports.

In the pre-North Sea oil era rapid periods of expansion were inevitably short-lived as the resulting balance of payments deficits forced successive governments to deflate the economy. Since 1981, however, the continued growth of manufactured imports has in effect been financed by North Sea oil and the economy has been allowed to expand unchecked by balance of payments constraints, albeit at a modest pace. As North Sea oil revenues decline, however, the balance of payments constraint on growth will return – unless, of course, manufacturing output and exports can be expanded to fill the gap left by oil. This objective, however, will require a major shift of resources into import substitution and export growth and, at present, there is little or no likelihood that such a shift will take place. In its absence the international competitiveness of manufacturing industry will continue to decline, and this implies a further contraction in manufacturing employment.

## SUMMARY

The notion that workers and their organizations are largely responsible for the present level of unemployment in Britain because they have priced themselves out of work does not throw much light on the causes of the problem nor does it provide a realistic basis for tackling it. By far the most important factor on the demand side of the labour market has been the contraction of industrial employment which, since 1979, has greatly exceeded the expansion of employment opportunities in services. Even if the service sector had expanded more rapidly it is doubtful if this would have significantly held back unemployment since there is an obvious and growing mismatch between the labour displaced from the industrial sector and the jobs available in services. The low level of productivity in British industry implies that there will be a further contraction in its employment base. It is therefore fundamentally implausible to argue that if the unemployed were prepared to accept jobs at lower wages, employers in the industrial sector would be inclined to create such jobs.

The contraction in industrial employment has been sharper in Britain since 1979 than in any other advanced industrial country and there is little evidence to suggest that this is simply part of a benign process of evolution into a 'post-industrial' society. By far the most important cause of the absolute fall in industrial, and particularly manufacturing, employment is declining international competitiveness. British industry's cost structure is uncompetitive primarily because of its low absolute level of productivity and its apparent inability to raise and sustain the underlying rate of productivity growth. Manufactured exports are, therefore, vulnerable both to exchange rate fluctuations and to increases in money wages which in turn lead to higher unit labour costs. Up to the late 1970s the upward pressure on domestic costs was largely offset by exchange rate depreciation. Since then, however, sterling has in varying degrees been over-valued against the currencies of key competitors and the balance of trade on manufactured goods has moved into substantial deficit. Britain is now a net importer of most types of manufactured goods, particularly of high value-added products, and it is difficult to see how lower real wages would do much to reverse this position.

In any event it is hard to imagine that the parties to collective bargaining would voluntarily reduce real wages except in the most exceptional circumstances. Although advocates of a de-centralized system of pay determination have in the past argued that this was the only way in which wages and productivity could be synchronized, the evidence to date suggests that such claims are ill-founded. Despite record levels of unemployment and changes in the framework of labour law which are commonly assumed to have brought about a much more even balance of bargaining power on the factory floor, average earnings are still rising faster than productivity. This in turn suggests that we should focus less attention on the alleged ability of over-mighty trade unions to price their members out of work as on the attitudes and behaviour of employers and, in particular, on the factors which have held down productivity.

# CHAPTER 4

## SOME EXPLANATIONS

*Though every great modern business bristles with problems of high intellectual as well as practical moment, physical, financial and administrative, how many responsible heads of business in this country possess any expert training in mechanics, finance, economics or psychology? The very notion of the need for such training appears to almost all of them a ridiculous pandering to intellectualism which unfits men for a real business life. Though a few of them are intelligent enough to recognise that Germany has got ahead of us in some profitable trades by employing scientific experts, and that the higher business training of young Americans is consistent with a rapid, lucrative career, very little has been done to secure for our industries the fruits of expert thinking and training.*

J. A. Hobson, 1922

In the previous chapter we focused on the tangible symptoms and most immediate causes of Britain's poor manufacturing performance and its impact on the structure of employment. To argue, however, that low productivity or poor non-price competitiveness is responsible for this level of performance does not take us very far. *Why* is the average level of British industrial productivity so low? *Why* has the relative performance of British industry, measured by the yardsticks of both price and non-price competitiveness, been so poor for so long? *Why* have many of the shortcomings in British entrepreneurship and industrial organization which were first noted by late Victorian observers proved to be so durable? Economists and economic historians still offer a variety of possible explanations. Some attribute Britain's industrial 'failure' to the influence of particular supply-side factors such as lack of investment, trade union militancy and poor entrepreneurship. Others have singled out excessive government spending and the unduly rapid growth of public service sector employment. Such hypotheses, while varying in emphasis, have one common feature insofar as they suggest that specific obstacles to industrial competitiveness can be removed by the 'right' policy measures.

Sceptics tend to point out, however, that although the pursuit of policies designed to improve manufacturing competitiveness and raise the general rate of economic growth has obsessed virtually every postwar government in Britain, the results have been, to say the least, disappointing. The relative ineffectiveness of government intervention is, they argue, due not so much to the allegedly variable and at times contradictory nature of industrial and economic policies but rather reflects a set of attitudes and beliefs which are embedded in society itself and, as such, are relatively unresponsive to specific policies. How else do we explain the fact that most foreign-owned manufacturing enterprises find it difficult or impossible to achieve in their British subsidiaries the standards of performance which they have achieved in other countries, even though these subsidiaries generally do better than their British-owned counterparts? There is, the sceptics say, a fundamental cultural hostility to industrial success in Britain which has starved industry of the best managerial talent, encouraged an anti-industrial bias within the educational system and produced an adversarial climate of labour relations on the factory floor.

To analyse fully these conflicting interpretations would be impossible in the space of one chapter. All we can hope to do is to discuss briefly the more important factors which are generally thought to have contributed to the related problems of low productivity, low output and poor international competitiveness. These include the growth of non-productive service employment, the level and quality of industrial investment, the management of the labour process and the role of education and training.

## TOO MANY DRONES IN THE HIVE?

In the previous chapter we commented critically on the assertion that the growth of service sector unemployment can be regarded as an effective substitute for employment in manufacturing. It was argued that, on the contrary, the expansion of the service sector as a whole is heavily dependent on the vitality of the industrial base. This general point forms the cornerstone of an interesting analysis put forward by Bacon and Eltis back in 1975. The crux of their argument is that successive British governments have expanded non-productive *public* service employment far in excess of the capacity of the productive sector of the economy to support it, with adverse consequences for the manufacturing base.[1]

They draw a clear distinction between the *market* sector of the economy, which produces the goods and services from which total consumption, investment and exports must be financed, and the *non-market* sector which supplies services financed by total tax revenues. The market sector is synonymous with private industries and services and includes those public corporations (for example steel, coal and electricity) which produce marketable goods. The non-market sector encompasses those services provided by central and local government. However necessary and desirable these public services may be, the fact that they are financed by tax revenues from the market sector of the economy means that their rate of growth must be compatible with the growth and profitability of this sector. Bacon and Eltis have argued that between 1961 and 1974 total employment in the non-market sector increased by over one-third relative to employment in the market sector and that this rate of growth was excessive. The rule that the non-market sector must be financed from the *surplus* created by the market sector was, therefore, broken. In Eltis' words:

A failure to finance the non-market sector from the surplus of the market sector can only result in balance of payments collapse as efforts are made to use the resources of foreigners to provide what a population is unwilling to pay for, or physical shortages of capital as a society consumes its seed-corn in the form of extra social services, and so fails to maintain the employment-creating capacity of its capital stock.[2]

Investment in the market sector of the economy, principally manufacturing, has therefore been 'crowded out' by the growth of the public service sector.

One obvious result of this excessive growth has been a corresponding rise in the tax burden on all employees throughout the economy, with adverse consequences for wage bargaining and industrial relations generally. As workers have seen their real take-home pay squeezed by income tax and National Insurance contributions, so they have tried to claw back the lost purchasing power through higher money wage settlements. The growth of public service employment is therefore seen as a major cause of the increasing trade union militancy and relatively high rates of inflation which characterized the period between 1968 and 1980. The underlying deterioration in the balance of trade on manufactured goods has also been ascribed to the expansion of the non-market sector. Import penetration has been increasing since the 1960s because non-market employment (at least up to 1980) continued to grow at all stages of the economic cycle. Profits, investment and output have all been squeezed by the overblown claims of the non-market sector, with the result that what little productivity growth has occurred has been at the expense of employment in manufacturing. Reversing the process of decline, therefore, implies both a much higher level of manufacturing productivity and a significantly smaller public service sector.

The Bacon and Eltis interpretation has gained much support since it was first published and since 1976 both the Callaghan and Thatcher governments have pursued policies which reflect at least some of its main propositions. As a *general* explanation of the contraction of the manufacturing sector, however, it does not hold up to critical scrutiny. Bacon and Eltis are certainly correct in drawing attention to the implications for wage bargaining of high and rising personal taxation. But their contention that British industry has performed badly *because* it has been starved of

both manpower and capital resources by the public service sector
is unconvincing.

A sceptical approach would distinguish between the crowding
out of *real* resources and *financial* 'crowding out'. In a fully
employed economy where all resources are being used, it is
obvious that if the government increases the public service
sector's share of the cake, some other sector must get less. But in
an economy with as much spare capacity, under-used capital and
unemployed manpower as Britain has had since the mid-1970s
and, more obviously, since 1980, the prospect of real resource
crowding out does not seem credible. While it is certainly true
that shortages of skilled manpower were a persistent source of
complaint by manufacturing employers during both the 1960s
and the 1970s, it is extremely unlikely that these were the result
of poaching by the non-market sector. Indeed, as we noted in
Chapter 2, much of the growth in both public and private service
employment took the form of jobs for women, often (and since
1980 almost exclusively) on a part-time basis. Conversely, much
of the manpower shaken out by the manufacturing sector since
the early 1970s has not been well matched, either occupationally
or geographically, with the vacancies available in public
services.

Financial 'crowding out', by contrast, could in theory occur at
any level of unemployment. The necessary conditions are, firstly,
a static money supply and velocity of circulation and, secondly,
a decision by the government to raise its own spending by increased borrowing rather than by putting up taxes. The prospect
of a bigger budget deficit will then drive up interest rates,
penalizing both private and corporate borrowers. This theory had
a strong deterrent effect on policy-makers after 1979 and helps
to explain why, despite vigorous lobbying from the business
community, the Thatcher government refused to countenance a
substantial increase in tax-financed capital spending as a
counter-cyclical measure even at the deepest point of the recession. A greater demand for investment funds by the government
would, it was argued, simply deprive the private sector of resources and damage the prospects of an investment-led recovery.

This theory does not, however, square with reality. Most industrial investment has traditionally been financed from internal sources and external funds can usually be acquired without great difficulty. While the cost of borrowing is obviously *one* of the factors influencing investment decisions, it is by no means the dominant influence. As the Treasury argued in its evidence to the Wilson Committee, the factor which above all others tends to determine investment decisions is the 'general macroeconomic climate' including, of course, the level of business confidence in future demand.[3] If industry has plenty of spare capacity, profits are depressed and businessmen are pessimistic about the future, then reductions in government borrowing and interest rates are unlikely *in themselves* to stimulate private investment – hence its extreme sluggishness during the cyclical upturn of 1981–4. In certain circumstances, however, a policy of fiscal expansion and higher government borrowing, which in turn stimulates the use of hitherto unused economic resources, may encourage a more optimistic climate and thereby stimulate industrial investment. This is precisely the lesson which was supposed to have been learned from the experience of the 1930s.

A final comment on the Bacon and Eltis thesis would be to refer back to Table 3 (p. 54) and point out that the growth of public service employment as a whole eased off and then came to a halt towards the end of the 1970s. With only one exception (health and social services), every major area of public service employment is now tending to contract and, in the light of known demographic trends, is likely to go on contracting. Despite this reduction the total tax burden in Britain increased from 36 per cent to nearly 40 per cent of GDP between 1979 and 1985, largely because of the need to finance a much higher level of unemployment than in the 1970s. This would seem to suggest that a policy of increasing government *capital* spending in order to reduce unemployment and improve the longer-term efficiency of the economic infrastructure might actually help to keep down the tax burden on individuals while raising the level of business confidence in the future of the British economy.

## TOO LITTLE INVESTMENT?

Another popular explanation of the low level of productivity in
British industry is based on the belief that the average worker
simply has less capital equipment at his elbow than his foreign
counterparts. Several studies, going back to the 1960s, have
emphasized the slow growth of British industry's capital stock
and have attributed this to the fact that Britain has consistently
invested a lower proportion of GDP than its major competitors.
In the 1960s Britain devoted slightly less than 18 per cent of
GDP to investment compared with an OECD average of about
21 per cent. During the 1970s Britain raised this proportion to
18·7 per cent while the OECD average increased to 22·2 per
cent. Japan, by contrast, has consistently invested more than 30
per cent of its GDP – and, of course, its productivity growth has
been much faster than Britain's. The assumption that more investment means faster growth has led to a critique of the role of
British financial institutions in providing funds for industrial
investment and underpins the belief, popular on the political
Left, that finance should be 'directed' into industry by a National
Investment Bank or some similar organization. This thesis is,
however, misguided. As Stout has observed, 'To prescribe for a
sluggish economy simply a larger slice of investment out of
output is rather like admonishing an aspiring but seriously out-
of-condition fell-runner to eat more heartily.'[4] Labour productivity depends not simply on the quantity of capital invested but
also and perhaps more especially on the composition of the capital stock, on how fully it is utilized, and on the extent to which it
embodies the most efficient techniques.

While aggregate investment as a proportion of GDP has
not changed very much over the years there has been a very
significant change in its composition. In the 1960s a very large
proportion of total fixed investment (over half at its peak in 1967)
was absorbed by the public sector, particularly in the form of
housing and other building projects. Since then there has been a
major shift in the distribution of investment funds towards the
private sector in general and in favour of plant, machinery and
transport in particular. This change in emphasis should, other

things being equal, have favoured productivity growth. There is certainly no evidence that Britain lags behind any of its major competitors, except Japan, in the proportion of GDP which it devotes to investment in plant, machinery and transport.[5] The mix of private sector investment has also changed, with services attracting a larger share of total expenditure and manufacturing claiming less – though this could be as much a consequence of the decline in manufacturing output and profits as a cause.

These changes in the composition of investment should have favoured productivity growth. The fact that the underlying rate of growth has *not* accelerated, however, suggests that our attention should be focused on the efficiency and quality of the investment which did take place. The fact that during the 1970s British industry's average capital–output ratio – the number of units of capital required to produce one unit of output – was rising while the real rate of return on capital was falling to disastrously low levels points in the same direction (Figure 15). Slow growth, particularly after 1973, was accompanied by much more widespread and pronounced margins of excess capacity than in the previous decade, despite the low level of investment.[6] By 1980 the output per unit of capital in West German, American and French manufacturing industry was between 2·7 and 2·3 times greater than in Britain.[7] If the quality and efficiency of investment are poor, the causes are likely to be found within industry itself rather than in any alleged deficiencies in the external supply of funds.

One important cause of relatively low returns lies in the nature of the investment which has taken place. Over the past twenty years British manufacturing investment has been increasingly biased in favour of asset *replacement* and *rationalization* as distinct from asset creation. This would in itself tend to depress the overall rate of return, but this effect seems to have been compounded by inefficiencies in the use of manpower and in factory organization. A report by the Central Policy Review Staff on the motor industry (1975), for example, found that with the same power at his elbow, and doing the same job, a continental car assembly worker normally produced twice as much as his British counterpart. This huge productivity differential was attributed to

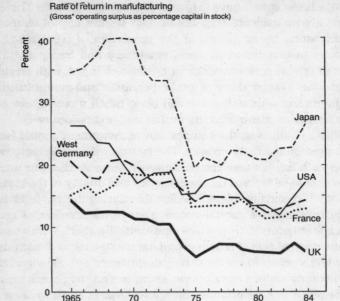

Figure 15   Rate of return in manufacturing. (Gross* operating surplus
            as % of gross capital stock.) (Source: *Economist*, 9 March
            1985.)

* Including stock appreciation.

overmanning (particularly in indirect support staff), slow pace of
production, quality faults, poor maintenance and heavy plant
overheads. Shortages of modern equipment, by contrast, were
thought to be only a minor cause of low productivity. Lower
nominal labour costs in Britain did not compensate for this
productivity gap.[8] While the motor industry may well have been
an extreme example of Britain's poor comparative productivity
in the 1970s, some of the reports produced by the various NEDC
Sector Working Parties in the second half of the decade yielded
similar evidence of inefficiency in the organization of the
manufacturing process. The improvement in the average return
on assets since 1980 has been less the result of new capital invest-

ment as of the widespread elimination of old, under-used plant and equipment, coupled with a massive shake-out of under-used manpower.

If, therefore, the main problem with British manufacturing investment is not that there is too little of it but that the real returns on it are too low, there is little point in berating the City of London for allegedly starving industry of funds. As Rose has pointed out, a study of financial systems around the world suggests that they tend to adapt themselves to industrial and commercial conditions. If other factors favour economic growth, 'finance' is unlikely to be a constraint.[9] The bulk of the evidence to the Wilson Committee (1980) suggested that the availability of external finance was not a significant independent constraint on private sector companies.[10] The House of Lords Select Committee also concluded that there was 'no shortage of money for investment for propositions that appear to be viable', although it noted several criticisms from the small-business sector of the cost and conditions of externally supplied finance.[11]

Historically it is certainly true that British banks have in general been far less involved in the provision of long-term investment funds for industry than their counterparts in West Germany and Japan. In Britain, however, the bulk of investment finance has traditionally been provided by manufacturing companies from their own internal resources, with the banks providing short-term funds only when required. Longer-term borrowing was, up to the 1970s, financed through debenture issues. With the onset of high rates of inflation after 1973, however, the cost of borrowing usually exceeded the real rate of return on assets, which virtually destroyed the debenture market. The banks responded by increasing their longer-term lending to industry, which helped to push the proportion of companies' external finance provided by these institutions to over 60 per cent by the beginning of the 1980s. This, however, was largely due to the recession and during the subsequent recovery the proportion of investment funds provided by the banks fell back sharply. At the time of writing nearly 75 per cent of company investment funds in the UK are provided from internal sources, supplemented by occasional issues of new equity.

While the banks as a whole are undoubtedly more attuned to the needs of industry than they were, they still do not hold shares in British firms, nor do they play an active role in the management of individual companies. This lack of direct involvement has often been compared unfavourably with the pro-active role of German and Japanese banks, the inference being that British companies typically lack this external source of pressure, backed by a supply of long-term funds, to invest in new products and techniques. In reality, however, external scrutiny of managerial performance takes place through the medium of investment analysts and institutional fund managers.

Over the past twenty years there has been a radical change in the structure of corporate share ownership in British industry. The proportion of shares owned by individuals fell from 58 per cent in 1963 to 25 per cent in 1983, while that owned by pension funds rose from 7 to 29 per cent and by insurance companies from 11 to 22 per cent over the same period.[12] Institutional shareholders now usually own the majority of shares in the larger manufacturing companies and have an obvious interest in the efficiency with which they are being managed. This does not necessarily imply that institutional shareholders give priority to short-term returns. On the contrary, they are likely to support well-planned programmes of innovation and growth provided that company managements take the trouble to communicate their plans to stockbrokers and investment analysts who influence institutional opinion. There is in fact far more support for British industry within the City of London than is often assumed. The extent to which this goodwill is actually tapped, however, depends in part on the ability of British companies to communicate effectively with City institutions and win their support for longer-term strategies. Until quite recently many manufacturing companies have adopted a defensive, inward-looking approach which has in times of crisis left them bereft of friends in both the City and the outside world in general. There is still considerable scope for improvement in these external communication skills.

## MAN MISMANAGEMENT?

If the main weakness of British industrial investment is its low
average productivity, our attention must be focused on those
factors at workplace level which are likely to discourage the
efficient use of capital equipment and manpower. The most popular targets for blame are still, of course, the trade unions. Just as
they are held responsible for the continuing strength of wage-
push in the economy, so it is claimed that their attachment to
old-fashioned restrictive practices is largely responsible for the
low level of productivity in British industry. The alleged con-
nection between trade unions and low productivity, however,
rests on two arguable propositions – firstly, that unilaterally
imposed *labour* practices are the most significant cause of inefficiency on the factory floor and, secondly, that it is the unions
themselves who are largely responsible for the existence and
retention of these practices. While not without some substance
in certain well-publicized work situations (for example Fleet
Street), as the basis for a *general* explanation of low productivity
neither of these propositions stands up to critical scrutiny.

There is a well-established body of comparative evidence going
back to the late Victorian era which suggests that British
manufacturing industry has consistently tolerated lower levels of
efficiency in the workplace than most foreign industries and
enterprises. The main conclusions of these comparative studies
are, firstly, that British manufacturing operations tend to be *over-
manned* in relation to the standards of manning comparable
equipment abroad. The use of skilled labour is relatively inefficient due to demarcation rules, while the numbers of indirect
and semi-skilled workers tend to be far higher than in foreign
enterprises. Secondly, even where manning levels are comparable, output is lower in British plants due to the relatively *slow
pace of work*. Machinery is customarily run at speeds below those
which it is technically capable of and does sustain in foreign
plants. Thirdly, manufacturing equipment in Britain tends to be
*poorly used* in other ways. Inadequate preventive maintenance
(despite relatively high levels of manning in maintenance functions), for example, tends to result in frequent breakdowns,

excessive downtime and low standards of quality requiring costly rectification.[13]

A survey of several industries in the West Midlands in the mid-1970s, for example, found widespread evidence of inefficiency in the manufacturing process. In medium-sized batch-production plants it was found that no more than 20 per cent of the time taken to process materials through the factory was spent productively. In these same factories neither labour nor plant was employed on directly productive work for more than an average of 50 per cent of the time available. The authors of this survey emphasized, however, that where machines were standing idle for over half the working day, the chief reponsibility lay not so much with a 'lazy' workforce as with incompetent *management*. Their conclusion is worth quoting: '. . . at a time when industrial viability is being undermined both by lack of ready cash and capital investment, increases in production of up to 100 per cent can be achieved by the more efficient utilisation of existing resources.' Alternatively, if the worst companies could have improved their performance to equal that of the best, output would have risen by 50 per cent.[14] Similarly, a comparative study in 1976 by the engineering construction industry's 'little Neddy' of British, American and European projects revealed that foreign projects were finished more quickly, were less prone to delay, were mostly executed with greater technical efficiency and required less labour. Once again this study emphasized the relationship between poor managerial organization and the relatively high level of non-productive time on British sites.[15] Other research has pointed to the relatively high average levels of overtime in British industry and has concluded that the relatively low sensitivity of overtime working to cyclical fluctuations in industrial output implies that much overtime is worked in order to augment earnings rather than production.[16]

It may of course be argued in defence of management that they might have been willing to introduce more efficient manufacturing methods and production technology if in the past the trade unions had been equally willing to negotiate sensible agreements on manning standards and working practices. Since the recession of the early 1980s, however, the combined effects of higher unemployment and reduced shop-floor militancy have enabled many managements to press ahead with these long-overdue improvements in efficiency. Proponents of this argument can point to some conspicuous examples of managerial success – notably in Fleet Street and the coal industry – which would not have been possible prior to the recession. Yet the currently sluggish trend in productivity growth seems to suggest that these well-publicized victories are by no means typical of manufacturing industry as a whole.

Indeed recent research suggests that the average productivity gap between British industry and its competitors in Japan, America and West Germany is still enormous. An important cause of this differential, however, is not so much the force of trade union resistance to change and innovation as the failure of employers to ensure that their workforces are adequately *trained* to make such change possible. A recent comparative survey (1985) by the NIESR, for example, of thirty-six manufacturing companies in the UK and West Germany found that labour productivity in the German plants was roughly 60 per cent higher than in the British factories.[17] This gap was not, however, attributed to differences in either manning levels or age of capital equipment but rather to the *capabilities* of the employees themselves. The survey reported firstly that about half the shop-floor workers in the German plants had apprentice-type qualifications, compared with a quarter in the UK. The second significant conclusion was that the financial rewards for skilled status were significantly higher in Germany. Thirdly, it was found that first-line supervisors and middle managers in the German plants were much more likely to have formal technical qualifications, whereas the tendency in Britain was to rely on 'practical experience'. The combined effect of these differences in education and training was to produce in Germany a more efficient, confident and innovative environment, in which breakdowns in the manufacturing process were less frequent and shorter and in which machinery tended to be more advanced and better maintained. These factors could explain at least a substantial part of the productivity gap.

The findings of this survey confirm the results of a study by

Prais in the late 1970s which found that, by comparison with manufacturing industry in Germany, British industry employs far fewer technically qualified staff at all levels. The gap is particularly wide in the intermediate ranges of the organizational hierarchy, where German companies are likely to employ broadly twice as many professionally qualified craftsmen, supervisors and technicians as their British counterparts. Prais concluded that, in addition to Germany's generally higher productivity, its productivity tends to be *relatively* higher in those industries that are skill-intensive, and particularly in those industries which rely on intermediate grades of skill. The competitive advantage of the German system of industrial education, based as it is on formal training and external examinations, is that by comparison with Britain it has provided a much greater stock of 'transferable' skills and techniques. In a world of rapid technological change this is without doubt a major competitive asset.[18] Comparative evidence from abroad, therefore, suggests that in seeking explanations for low productivity in British industry we should focus less attention on the activities of trade unions *per se* and more on those inputs to the organization of production which fall primarily within the control of management. Arguably the most important supply-side factor is the quality and flexibility of the labour force, including management itself, and this in turn underlines the significance of education and training.

## AN UNTRAINED ARMY?

Over the past two or three years there has been a growing awareness in Britain of the crucial link between education, training and industrial performance. A Green Paper on Higher Education issued in 1985, for example, emphasized the government's concern

... that our competitors are producing, and plan in the future to produce, more qualified scientists, engineers, technologists and technicians than the United Kingdom. A thriving economy needs these skills both to develop the talents of entrepreneurs and to support their achievements: if the present trends continue, the result seems likely to be a further fall in our relative standard of living and our ability to sustain our cultural heritage.[19]

Official recognition that British industrial competitiveness is being held back by shortages of qualified manpower is welcome but belated. As with so much else in the current debate about the future prospects for British manufacturing industry, the evidence of relative failure in education and training goes back to the late nineteenth century. By comparison with Germany, Britain has historically placed little emphasis on the provision of full-time education in subjects such as engineering and other related disciplines which have a direct and practical relevance to industrial growth. The reasons for this neglect would in themselves occupy a book. At the risk of over-simplification, however, there can be little doubt that the failure of the industrial revolution to transform the pre-industrial values of British society has played a major role. In the words of one recent study:

Elite educational institutions from the Victorian era reflected and propagated an anti-industrial bias. The genteel pattern of the later Victorian public school was fixed (one level lower) on the new state grammar schools from their establishment by the Education Act of 1902. Similarly, the ancient universities served as a powerful model for state-provided higher education in the twentieth century ... Technological education made slow headway. Manufacturers aspiring to the status of full-fledged gentlemen recognised that engineering was not a suitable career for such a goal. Consequently they did not seek it for their sons ... Thus, engineering was left to the sons of the skilled working class.[20]

Any discussion of the specific failures of the British system of industrial training, and particularly its apparent inability to produce qualified engineers and technicians on the German scale, must therefore begin with the traditional approach to education in Britain. Several studies have emphasized that secondary-school education is still more academic and specialized in Britain than elsewhere and that the system of 'O' and 'A' levels sets a premium on academic as opposed to practical achievement. Moreover, the typical secondary-school curriculum is still unduly biased in favour of arts, pure science and other subjects which are not obviously geared to the world of work. As a result the output of the secondary system falls into two broad categories – a minority who are qualified to progress into higher education and a much larger proportion who leave school without qualifications or any alternative form of vocational preparation. The German system, by contrast, provides a broad curriculum, combined with significantly higher levels of attainment in subjects such as mathematics, and more pre-vocational instruction with a clear industrial and commercial bias. The result is that far fewer young people leave the German school system without qualifications than in Britain, and the German emphasis on applied studies ensures that industry can draw on a better-educated and more immediately employable stock of manpower.

Excessive specialization in British secondary schools carries over into the higher-education sector. Despite several attempts since the 1950s to increase the output of graduate engineers and technologists, most notably by creating new technology-based universities and polytechnics, the British system still seems incapable of coming anywhere near the numbers produced in many competitor countries. In Britain around 12,000 engineers graduate from the higher education system each year, compared with 30,000 in France and 80,000 in Japan.[21] Even allowing for differences in population there is no doubt that engineering and related subjects are heavily under-represented in British universities. Equally important, in Britain engineering has traditionally been taught as an academic subject rather than a vocational one, and the completion of professional training has been left largely to employers. The output of engineering graduates is inadequate both in relation to that of major international competitors and to the needs of British industry itself. In recent years there has been a stream of complaints from British employers about the shortage of graduates in key growth areas of engineering such as electronics and manufacturing systems. It is largely in response to this lobbying and publicity that the government has at last recognized that positive steps should be taken not simply to increase the flow of suitably qualified graduates into industry but, more generally, to tackle the root causes of the shortfall which lie deep within the education system and its traditional values.

This in turn suggests that industry itself must bear much of the responsibility for the historical neglect of professional education in engineering and related subjects. The fundamental problem, noted by successive commentators over many years but so far unresolved – is the low status accorded to engineers by British society. The reason why this problem should exist at all – remarkably, it might be supposed, in a country which once prided itself on being 'the workshop of the world' – is not so much the anti-industrial culture of the British educational establishment as the anti-educational bias of generations of British employers. Ever since the days of the 'heroic', self-made entrepreneur, British industry has tended to draw most of its skilled manpower from within its own ranks. Craftsmen and, ultimately, many senior managers have been recruited through the system of shop-floor apprenticeship, topped up where necessary by part-time technical education in local institutions. Formal, professional education and training has been regarded with suspicion and 'book-learning' viewed as incompatible with the 'practical' needs of industry.

While these traditional attitudes may have started to change over the past decade or so, there still seems to be a wide gap between Britain and its major industrial competitors in terms of the ability of industry to attract highly qualified, technically based graduates into managerial jobs. Senior managers in West German, Japanese and French industry are much more likely to have formal qualifications in engineering and related subjects, gained in elite educational establishments, than their British counterparts. These differences in educational attainment and social background have in turn influenced the way in which managerial effectiveness is appraised. Several studies of management attitudes in Britain have emphasized that 'Expertise is defined in terms of personal characteristics rather than technical competence, and the management function becomes one of leading or managing people and seeking promotion, rather than producing a product.'[22]

These observed differences in the professional status and qualifications of British managers relative to their major competitors have also influenced attitudes towards training and retraining the industrial workforce. Despite over two decades of almost continuous public discussion of the shortage of skilled man-power in Britain, and various attempts by successive govern-ments to tackle this problem, a recent survey conducted for the Manpower Services Commission and NEDO suggests that the typical approach to training in British industry is still grossly inadequate by the best international standards. By comparison with West Germany and Japan, where training is well embedded in enterprise cultures, many British companies still regard spending on training as an overhead cost rather than an invest-ment linking directly to future profitability. This implies that training in British industry is not a steady, sustained activity but rather fluctuates with the business cycle. Other findings from this survey tend to confirm the conclusion that many senior managers regard training as a relatively low priority and are generally unaware of the contribution which this activity makes to the competitiveness of their foreign rivals. Consequently, despite the general absence of qualitative yardsticks by which British managers can judge their spending on training, most companies covered by the survey seemed to believe that their current provision in this area was either 'about right' or 'above average'.[23]

Such attitudes do not augur well for the international com-petitiveness of British industry. In recent years technological change in manufacturing has focused not only on product design but also, and increasingly, on the production process itself. There has in many cases been a decisive break with the traditional technology of high standardized volumes and much more flexible, automated manufacturing systems are now being rapidly adopted. Such systems, often based on Japanese practices, enable companies to respond much more quickly to the changing needs of customers and require far fewer indirect workers and much lower stock levels. Since it is estimated that in British industry over £20 billion is currently tied up in stocks and work-in-progress, any change in manufacturing systems which enables managements to reduce this huge investment is likely to have a positive effect on profitability. The new systems also facilitate major improvements in labour productivity which, as we noted in the previous chapter, is British industry's biggest single competitive weakness. For our purposes, however, the key point is that the introduction of new manufacturing technology typically requires a major investment in training and retraining employees at all levels in the organization – management, supervisors and craftsmen – as a pre-condition of its effective use. Unless, therefore, British industry achieves a step-change in its approach to training it will continue to fall behind its major international competitors.


## SUMMARY

The major cause of low productivity in British industry is not attributable primarily to the alleged shortage of capital investment but rather to a failure on the part of successive generations of British managers to make effective use of the resources, human as well as financial, at their disposal. This failure emerges in several ways – in the inefficient organization of the production process, in widespread overmanning, poor cost control and, above all, in the employment of an ill-educated and inadequately trained workforce. While trade union recalcitrance may well have contributed to the retention of inefficient working practices, the primary responsibility for their existence lies squarely with management. Trade unions tend to react to the working environment in which their members find themselves and take their cue from the managers with whom they deal from day to day. It is management which sets the standard of performance and organizes all the resources of the enterprise to achieve it. If British management has fallen behind its major competitors in discharging these basic functions the reasons must be sought in the professionalism and technical competence of those who call themselves managers. This in turn points towards certain well-attested educational, social and cultural peculiarities which the profession of industrial management in Britain has historically exhibited. While these peculiarities may be diminishing, the gap which now separates the performance of British manufacturing industry as a whole from that of its major competitors is such that faster progress is essential.

The foregoing analysis clearly implies that a further contraction in Britain's industrial employment base is almost certain, with obvious consequences for the overall level of unemployment. The necessary drive to improve productivity, based on the application of new manufacturing systems, will undoubtedly result in further job losses, but if this process results in a strengthening of the international competitiveness of British industry – with all that this would imply for the balance of payments, real incomes and inflation – it will increase the capacity of the economy as a whole to generate new employment. If, by contrast, industrial competitiveness does not improve, the number of jobs lost in manufacturing will be even greater and the ability of other sectors of the economy to replace them will be correspondingly reduced.

# CHAPTER 5

# THE CASUALTIES

*After all allowance has been made for special cases, the selective influence of personal character stands out as one of the dominant facts of the situation. Every employer, where he has the choice, dismisses the less satisfactory workmen and keeps the more satisfactory. In every organized trade the more regular and more efficient men have to pay for the less efficient and less regular. Almost inevitably, again, irregularity of employment reacts upon the man and accentuates the weaknesses with which he started. The net result is that the unemployed at any time, though they may include men of every grade, are as a whole below the general level in the qualities that make for industrial efficiency. The bulk of them are in no sense unemployable. They are equally removed from being the picked men of their trades. They are simply, taken in the mass, less competent, less industrious, less temperate or less regular than their fellows who have retained employment.*

W. H. Beveridge, 1909

It was argued in Chapter 2 that most of those who are currently on the unemployment register are not there by choice. Some workers, however, are more likely to enter unemployment than others and, indeed, exhibit certain well-known characteristics. By age, the young and the old are over-represented in the stock of the unemployed; by occupation, unskilled manual workers are heavily over-represented; by sex and family status, single men and men with large families are over-represented. A worker's chances of entering unemployment are also influenced by the industry or sector in which he works and the area in which he lives. In other words, the composition of the stock of unemployed at any given time is determined by a selection process which varies in its severity according to the level of demand for labour. In a period of generally low unemployment, marked by only minor fluctuations in demand, the composition of the

unemployed stock is likely to be heavily weighted towards the
most marginal elements in the labour force. Between 1970 and
1974, for example, some 19 per cent of the labour force accounted for *all* spells of registered unemployment, with half these
spells attributable to only 3 per cent of the workforce.[1] Since
1974, however, and more particularly since 1980, the demand
for most types of labour has fallen sharply. Many employers have
been obliged to shake out or shut out marginal and core labour
alike. The composition of the unemployed stock has, as a result,
moved closer to the composition of the labour force itself.

A second process then determines the length of time that
workers stay on the register. The stringency of this process is
also strongly influenced by the general level of demand. The
lower the level of unemployment, the higher the proportion of
unemployed who remain on the register for short spells and vice
versa. The reason for this is self-evident. In a market where many
workers are chasing few vacancies, employers are likely to raise
their recruitment standards so that the more marginal applicants
for jobs are automatically rejected. Moreover, in a period of
rapidly rising unemployment such as 1980–82 there is likely to
be a significant flow of redundant workers on to local unemployment registers. Some of these workers are likely to be
relatively old and unskilled, but others may be young, skilled
and adaptable. Those who fall into the second category will then
compete for whatever vacancies are available in the local market
with workers who are already on the register. To the extent that
they compete successfully, they are said to *displace* other unemployed workers who might otherwise have obtained work and
whose stay on the register is thereby prolonged. The likelihood of
widespread displacement will obviously be greater in labour
markets which are dominated by a small number of employers
and in which the level of unemployment is already high.

Can the problem of unemployment in Britain today, therefore,
be described as one of 'particular people' in 'particular places'? If
so, then an appropriate remedial strategy would place considerable emphasis on measures to improve the employment prospects of those individuals and groups who are over-represented
in the stock of the unemployed. Policies to encourage the

creation of jobs in localities of exceptionally high unemployment would also be consistent with this approach. An induced expansion of aggregate demand, however, particularly in the absence of supply-side policies to improve training and encourage labour mobility, would not be an appropriate response. But while it is still the case that some workers are more likely to enter and remain in unemployment than others, the spread of unemployment from the marginal to the core groups in the labour market and the persistence of some conspicuous mismatches between the unemployed and vacancies indicates a more fundamental change in the demand for labour. The current recession simply accelerated longer-term changes in the structure of employment which at any level of aggregate demand will be associated with relatively high rates of unemployment.

Who, then, are the unemployed?


## THE OLDER WORKER

Most published analyses of unemployment underline the importance of *age* as a factor influencing both a worker's chances of entering unemployment and the length of time he spends on the register. Beveridge, for example, emphasized both the vulnerability of the older worker to displacement by new technology and the difficulties he could expect to encounter in the search for new employment.[2] Daniel has stressed the age factor even more strongly:

> ... if there is one rule it is that, among workers who lose their jobs, the older they are, the more difficulty they have in finding a new job, the longer their period out of work, and the more inferior any new job is likely to be to the one they lost. Equally, the older a worker is, the less he is likely to retrain or move to find another job. The influence of age is overwhelming. It is far more important than jobs in the labour market, or skill, or qualifications.[3]

Other studies, however, suggest that age relative to *skill* might be the most significant influence on entry to and duration of unemployment.

Employers who, due to adverse market conditions, find themselves obliged to achieve substantial reductions in manpower costs normally try to shake out those workers who have the lowest productivity relative to their earnings and those with poor health records or some physical incapability. Most of those who are selected for redundancy on such criteria tend to be relatively old and unskilled. In his study of redundancies in the West Midlands engineering industry in 1966–8, for example, Mackay found that those made redundant 'tended to be older employees with long periods of service who were not particularly suited, in terms of skill, to overcome these disadvantages in looking for new jobs'. The minority of Mackay's sample who never got another job were composed of men in the over-fifty-five age group.[4] In these circumstances a lengthy period of service with one employer, far from being a positive asset to the worker in his search for a new job, may make it much harder for him to adapt to new terms and conditions of employment. As Beveridge noted in his prewar study, 'Prolonged continuity of employment with one firm is apt to make a man peculiarly helpless when that one firm dismisses him or fails. He has no previous experience in looking for work; he has no personal connections with other employers or foremen; at a time of general depression he often goes under completely and rapidly when men of a more casual habit survive.'[5]

It might be thought that older workers with long service would enjoy relatively strong protection against redundancy under 'last in, first out' arrangements and that their chances of entering unemployment would therefore be less than those of other workers. This does not, however, seem to be the case. The availability of relatively attractive lump-sum redundancy payments for long-service employees, the possibility of early retirement and the natural reluctance of older workers to risk refusing an apparently generous offer all help to explain why they are more likely to enter unemployment than any but those in the under-twenty-five group. The authors of an MSC study of redundancies at the Firestone Tyre and Rubber Company in 1980, for example, found that slightly over half of all those declared redundant were over fifty years old and that 68 per cent were previously in unskilled or semi-skilled jobs.[6] In his earlier survey Daniel reported that 42 per cent of the unemployed in the over-fifty-five group had been made redundant compared with only 17 per cent of those under twenty-five.[7]

Many older workers in managerial and professional jobs may decide to take early retirement on relatively favourable terms (i.e. lump sums and good pensions) and then cease to be interested in finding another full-time job. Older workers in unskilled or semi-skilled manual jobs, by contrast, may be compelled to enter unemployment with little more to live on than their social security income, supplemented perhaps by a modest redundancy payment. Such workers may be anxious to get another job but find it virtually impossible to do so. The strong and well-known association between age and duration of unemployment has emerged from successive surveys. It is generally accepted that both the prospects of getting work and keenness to get work decline in *all* age groups as the duration of unemployment increases. Male workers over fifty-five, however, are less likely than any other group to have good or reasonable prospects of obtaining work at the outset of their entry into unemployment; after a few months on the register only a very small minority are still likely to have such prospects.[8] As a result, in the late 1970s roughly one-third of those who had been on the register for a year or more were over fifty-five years of age.

Over the next few years, however, as long-term unemployment increased in all age groups, the relative significance of the over-fifty-five age group declined. By 1985 this group accounted for only 15 per cent of those on the register who had been unemployed for over a year (see Table 4).

## THE YOUNG WORKER

Changes in youth unemployment are closely related to changes in total unemployment, but move with greater amplitude. Why should this be so? The obvious explanation is that in a recession most employers respond to falling demand and growing pressure on manpower costs by curtailing recruitment and reducing employment through natural wastage. The effect of such

**Table 4** Male unemployment by age and duration, April 1980 and April 1985

| Unemployed in each age group as a percentage of all unemployed | Age group: | | | | |
|---|---|---|---|---|---|
| April 1980 | Under 25 | 25–45 | 45–55 | 55+ | Total |
| Under one month | 44·6 | 35·4 | 9·6 | 10·4 | 100 |
| One to 6 months | 32·8 | 38·9 | 14·4 | 13·9 | 100 |
| 6 to 12 months | 28·5 | 35·6 | 12·1 | 23·8 | 100 |
| 12 to 24 months | 18·5 | 34·2 | 14·7 | 32·6 | 100 |
| Over 24 months | 6·9 | 29·3 | 21·4 | 42·4 | 100 |

Total registered male unemployment = 1,010,975

| April 1985 | Under 25 | 25–45 | 45–55 | 55+ | Total |
|---|---|---|---|---|---|
| Under one month | 40·2 | 37·8 | 11·1 | 10·9 | 100 |
| One to six months | 40·7 | 38·1 | 10·8 | 10·4 | 100 |
| 6 to 12 months | 41·7 | 34·6 | 10·5 | 13·2 | 100 |
| 12 to 24 months | 31·7 | 40·3 | 14·2 | 13·8 | 100 |
| Over 24 months | 18·7 | 46·2 | 19·5 | 15·6 | 100 |

Total registered male unemployment = 2,270,721

(Source: *Employment Gazette*, May 1980 and May 1985.)

measures is likely to fall mainly on young people who are either joining the labour market or changing their jobs fairly frequently. The more severe the recession, the more complete the shut-out of young people is likely to be – hence the rise in youth unemployment rates in 1975–7 and the much sharper increases since 1979.[9] The effects of falling demand are likely to be compounded if the supply of new entrants to the labour market is simultaneously increasing, as indeed it has been since the early 1970s. Between 1974 and 1981 the number of males in the labour force aged between sixteen and nineteen grew by 291,000 (28 per cent) and the number of females in the same category increased by 303,000 (36 per cent).[10] Given this combination of increasing supply and falling demand, it is hardly surprising that youth unemployment rates have risen so sharply in recent years. Nor is it surprising that, given the same combination of demand and supply-side factors, youth unemployment is now much higher throughout Western Europe than it was in the 1970s.

Some observers have pointed out that youth unemployment in the UK has risen more sharply since 1979 than in most other Western countries and, as a proportion of the young labour force, is now surpassed only by the Italian rate. This may simply reflect the fact that the *total* unemployment rate is currently higher in the UK than in most other Western countries. It has also been argued, however, that changes in the relative earnings of young people in the UK have priced them out of jobs that they might otherwise have had. Comparisons have been made between the British and German apprenticeship systems in order to 'prove' that German employers provide more jobs for young people than their British counterparts because the cost of employing them is relatively low.[11] It must be emphasized, however, that German apprentices are paid not merely to work but to be trained through day-release courses, whereas in Britain those young people who are hired are much more likely to be given full-time work with little or no systematic training. Nor is there any evidence to suggest that the relative earnings of young people in the UK have changed significantly since the early 1970s. In 1980 a male under eighteen could expect to earn 39 per cent of the average male adult rate, rising to 68 per cent by age twenty, which was virtually the same structure of relative earnings as in 1976. The corresponding figures for young females were 55 and 79 per cent, again with no change between 1976 and 1980.[12]

The absence of any significant changes in the relative earnings of young people which might explain the rise in youth unemployment since the mid-1970s does not, of course, exclude the possibility that their real wages are still above their market-clearing level. If this is the case, then any recovery in the demand for labour is likely to benefit men and women in the prime age groups. Consequently the previously observed tendency for youth unemployment to fall rapidly during cyclical upswings may not emerge. There is some evidence, admittedly anecdotal, to support the claim that many employers are extremely reluctant to hire young people when more mature and experienced workers are available. The relative cost of employing young people, however, is by no means the only factor likely to influence the demand for them. A survey by the MSC in 1976, for example, found that many employers were critical of the general standards of school-leavers, particularly their attitude to work, their lack of numeracy and literacy and their general behaviour.[13] A more recent (1981) survey by the CBI confirms that there is a widespread belief among employers that young people are 'poor value for money'.[14] If this is the case we may speculate that only a very substantial reduction in the real cost of employing young people, sufficient to offset the negative characteristics perceived by employers, is likely to have much impact on youth unemployment in the foreseeable future. Unless such measures are adopted in the context of a general increase in the demand for labour, they will simply reduce unemployment among young people at the expense of the prime age groups.

Finally, we must note that while the sharp increase in youth unemployment rates since 1980 could have been predicted from the past relationship between youth and total unemployment, the growing gap between the rate at which young people enter unemployment and the rate at which they leave it has brought about a significant change in the character of the problem. Although the likelihood of entry into unemployment was for many young people greater in the second half of the 1970s than in the early part of the decade, the length of their spells on the register was typically short. The number of young people on the register reflected, in the words of one report, 'fairly short but frequent periods of unemployment rather than the inability of the young to find any kind of work'.[15] In July 1977, for example, barely 20 per cent of registrants in the under-twenty-five age group had been unemployed for more than six months. In July 1981 some 34 per cent of the under-twenty-five group fell into this category and by July 1985 this had risen to 50 per cent. Using a stricter measure of long-term unemployment, the upward trend is even sharper. In July 1977 only 7·5 per cent of registrants under twenty-five had been unemployed for more than one year; by July 1981 some 13 per cent of young registrants fell into this

category and in July 1985 the proportion reached 28 per cent.
As Table 4 above indicates, during the early 1980s the under-
twenty-five age group accounted for a significant and growing
proportion of the long-term unemployed. Since for most people
the chances of getting employment decline as their spell on the
register lengthens, there must now be a real possibility that a
significant minority of those young people who are currently
unemployed will remain unemployed for the rest of their lives.


## THE UNSKILLED, UNQUALIFIED WORKER

At every stage in the economic cycle there is an oversupply of
unskilled, unqualified labour. This is by no means a new
phenomenon. In his 1909 study, for example, Beveridge
observed: 'The glut of labour in the unskilled and unorganized
occupations is notorious. Has there ever, in the big towns at
least, been a time when employers could not practically get at a
moment's notice all the labourers they required?'[16] Unskilled and
semi-skilled manual workers have been heavily and consistently
over-represented among the unemployed throughout the postwar
period. Between 1959 and 1973 workers described by the Department of Employment as 'general labourers' constituted more
than half the stock of unemployed, although they comprised
only about one-quarter of the working population. Since 1973
the share of this group in total unemployment has fallen to about
20 per cent as other occupational groups have been affected
by the rise in unemployment. Nevertheless they remain over-
represented in the unemployed stock and, in particular, in the
long-term unemployed. Assuming that the bulk of them are in-
voluntarily unemployed, this seems to suggest that there is a
persistent lack of demand for unskilled labour. Low vacancies/
unemployment ratios for general labourers confirm this conclusion (Table 5).

The fact that notified vacancies only cover about a third of
total vacancies at any given time means that too much emphasis
should not be placed on the V/U ratio for any occupational group.
Nevertheless, Table 5 underlines the continued deterioration in

**Table 5**  Vacancies/unemployment ratios for broad occupational groups

| Occupational group | March 1975: | | | March 1978: | | | March 1982: | | |
|---|---|---|---|---|---|---|---|---|---|
| | Registered unemployed | Notified vacancies | V/U ratio | Registered unemployed | Notified vacancies | V/U ratio | Registered unemployed | Notified vacancies | V/U ratio |
| Managerial and professional | 48,810 | 22,095 | 0·45 | 104,286 | 16,781 | 0·16 | 252,773 | 14,782 | 0·05 |
| Clerical and related | 99,265 | 24,523 | 0·24 | 186,861 | 28,586 | 0·15 | 339,955 | 17,320 | 0·05 |
| Other non-manual | 29,795 | 13,966 | 0·46 | 76,712 | 15,506 | 0·20 | 173,848 | 14,739 | 0·09 |
| Craft and similar occupations | 93,382 | 43,934 | 0·47 | 160,983 | 48,246 | 0·29 | 404,457 | 15,247 | 0·03 |
| General labourers | 274,043 | 30,648 | 0·11 | 465,537 | 9,606 | 0·02 | 806,047 | 3,563 | 0·004 |
| Other manual occupations | 199,057 | 42,858 | 0·21 | 321,730 | 65,448 | 0·20 | 715,726 | 38,045 | 0·05 |
| Total: all occupations | 744,352 | 178,024 | 0·23 | 1,316,109 | 184,173 | 0·13 | 2,692,806 | 103,696 | 0·03 |

(Source: *Department of Employment Gazette*, various issues.)

the market position of the unskilled. The term 'unskilled' also covers those school-leavers and other young workers who have no formal qualifications and who, as we noted above, now constitute a significant proportion of the long-term unemployed. A survey of the long-term unemployed in 1979, for example, found that only a minority had any formal educational or vocational qualifications. About three-quarters of the sample had no qualifications of any kind and a significant minority had literacy or language problems. The absence of qualifications was almost as marked among the young unemployed in the sample as among the older age groups.[17] This disturbing feature clearly underlines the need for measures such as the government's Youth Training Scheme, designed to prepare the bulk of school-leavers for employment. It also confirms the general criticisms made in the previous chapter of the apparent inability of the present system of secondary education in Britain to prepare a large proportion of its output for employment.

The growth of long-term unemployment among unskilled and semi-skilled male manual workers is symptomatic of a fundamental shift in the structure of *employment* away from manual occupations as a whole. Non-manual jobs rose from just over one-third of total employment in 1961 to nearly half in 1978. During the same period manual employment contracted on average by about 1 per cent a year, with sharper falls in jobs for supervisors/foremen, 'non-transferable' craftsmen and general labourers. Structural changes within the mining and manufacturing sector as a whole are estimated to have extinguished about one million *craft* jobs over this period in addition to all those in less skilled grades.[18] Although shortages of certain types of craftsmen continued to be reported during the 1970s, the market for most skilled manual workers was significantly easier at the end of the decade than at the beginning. During the ensuing recession, the demand for all types of labour fell, while a survey of industrialists conducted by the NIESR in early 1982 found that shortages of skilled manual labour had virtually disappeared. Significantly, however, many of the respondents felt that they still had excess labour, particularly excess unskilled labour.[19] Since then, of course, shortages of skilled manpower

have re-emerged, although many of the occupations involved
are now non-manual.

## THE FEMALE WORKER

As female activity rates have risen, so has registered unemployment among women. Although a minority of women who
are unemployed still do not register, the female propensity to
register is much higher now than in the early 1970s. Of the 4·8
million inflows on to the register in 1984, just over 2 million
were women, while of the 4·5 million outflows, some 1·6 million
were women. Between 1980 and 1985 female registered unemployment rose by 96 per cent compared with an 86 per cent
rise among men, although the rate of female unemployment
remained well below that for men (9·4 per cent in 1984
compared with 15·7 per cent).

Does this imply, therefore, that relatively high female unemployment will become a permanent feature of the British
labour market, as it already is in most other West European
labour markets? It has been suggested that the continuing shortage of employment for men will induce many of them to compete
for jobs which have been customarily occupied by women. It has
even been argued that employers should be discouraged from
hiring women, particularly married women, because a reduction
in male unemployment should take 'priority'. Exponents of this
view, however, seriously underestimate the continuing force and
extent of occupational segregation in Britain. Despite legislative
attempts to promote equal pay and equal employment opportunities for women, they still occupy more of the lower-paid,
lower-status jobs with limited career prospects than men. The
expansion of the service sector since the 1960s has created many
such jobs and is likely to create more of them. It is difficult to
envisage any significant or widespread dismantling of these well-
established barriers to interchangeability between men and
women.

The future growth of employment opportunities for women
could, however, be held back by the continued application of

microprocessor technology. In any service where large amounts of relatively simple information are handled, considerable cost savings are likely to be derived from the displacement of manual methods by microprocessor technology. Since much of this labour has hitherto been provided by women, they are particularly vulnerable to the employment consequences of technological change.[20] It may well be, therefore, that the structural shift away from unskilled manual employment for men which we noted above is already being complemented by a similar fall in the demand for unskilled female labour. One symptom of this trend may well be the convergence of the unemployment rates among women under twenty with the rates of men in the same age group. This suggests that the employment prospects of young, unskilled and unqualified women are now as bad as those of their male counterparts, and are likely to remain so.

## REGIONAL AND LOCAL UNEMPLOYMENT

A well-known characteristic of unemployment is that it consistently affects some regions of Britain more than others, although the extent to which it does so is now far less than during the inter-war period. In 1936, for example, unemployment rates in Scotland, the North-East and the North-West were about three times, and in Wales nearly five times, the rate in London and the South-East.[21] Throughout the postwar period regional unemployment rates were much less dispersed and moved even closer together after the recession of 1975–7 (Table 6). The reasons for this convergence are well known. During the inter-war period unemployment was heavily concentrated in those regions where the structure of employment was dominated by traditional export industries. In regions and areas where employment was more diversified and where newer manufacturing industries had been established, unemployment rates were relatively low at all stages of the economic cycle. Since 1945, however, regional rates have been much less dispersed whether demand has been high or low. Although the postwar boom affected some regions more than others, all regions felt some

**Table 6 Regional male unemployment rates (Great Britain)**

| Region | 1968* Rate | 1968* As % of GB | 1977 Rate | 1977 As % of GB | 1979 Rate | 1979 As % of GB | 1981 Rate | 1981 As % of GB | 1985 Rate | 1985 As % of GB |
|---|---|---|---|---|---|---|---|---|---|---|
| South-East | 2·1 | 67 | 5·7 | 78 | 4·6 | 69 | 10·0 | 74 | 11·7 | 73 |
| East Anglia | 2·3 | 74 | 6·4 | 87 | 5·4 | 81 | 11·1 | 82 | 11·9 | 75 |
| West Midlands | 2·6 | 83 | 6·7 | 91 | 6·3 | 95 | 16·2 | 120 | 18·0 | 113 |
| East Midlands | 2·4 | 77 | 6·0 | 82 | 5·5 | 83 | 12·3 | 91 | 14·9 | 94 |
| Yorkshire & Humberside | 3·4 | 109 | 6·8 | 93 | 6·6 | 100 | 14·6 | 108 | 17·7 | 111 |
| North-West | 3·3 | 106 | 9·0 | 123 | 8·4 | 127 | 16·6 | 123 | 19·9 | 125 |
| South-West | 2·9 | 93 | 8·3 | 113 | 6·7 | 101 | 11·9 | 88 | 13·6 | 85 |
| North | 6·3 | 103 | 9·5 | 130 | 9·9 | 150 | 18·0 | 133 | 23·0 | 144 |
| Scotland | 4·5 | 145 | 9·5 | 130 | 9·0 | 136 | 16·0 | 118 | 19·1 | 120 |
| Wales | 4·8 | 154 | 9·2 | 126 | 8·7 | 131 | 17·1 | 126 | 20·5 | 129 |
| | | | | | | | | | | |
| Great Britain | 3·1 | | 7·3 | | 6·6 | | | | | |

*September figures only.
(Source: *Department of Employment Gazette*, various issues.)

benefit in terms of lower unemployment rates. Where structural problems were identified in particular regional economies, as they were in the case of the north, Scotland and Merseyside, governments sought to achieve a more equal distribution of employment opportunities by encouraging firms to move there from regions of very low unemployment.

During the post-1974 recession, however, and particularly after 1979, virtually every manufacturing industry was severely affected by falling demand, irrespective of location. The West Midlands, with its heavy dependence on motor vehicles and related industries, was particularly hard hit and its un-employment rate rose sharply relative to the national average. The South-East retained its traditional position as the region with the lowest rate, although this moved significantly closer to the national average after 1977. This probably reflects the decline of manufacturing industry in the Greater London area and the fail-ure of service employment to expand rapidly enough to offset these job losses.[22] East Anglia and the East Midlands also moved closer to the national average during the 1970s, although the former still stayed comfortably below it. The South-West greatly improved its relative performance between 1977 and 1982, pos-sibly because its relatively small manufacturing base contracted less rapidly than elsewhere while its performance in the service sector remained strong. Scotland remained above the national average but less so than in the 1970s. Unemployment in York-shire and Humberside reverted to the relative position it occupied in the late 1960s after a temporary improvement in the mid-1970s, while both the North and the North-West stayed well above their 1968 position (Table 6). The significance of declining industries in the employment structures of these regions almost certainly explains the behaviour of their relative unemployment rates.

The convergence of regional unemployment rates since the 1960s, combined with a structural shift away from unskilled employment and the growth of long-term unemployment among men, tends to confirm the 'structuralist' argument that 'a person's prospects in the labour market now depend almost as much on his occupational group and his age as on the area in which he lives'.[23] Yet within most regions there are still some conspicuous discrepancies between *local* unemployment rates. In his analysis of unemployment in the 1930s Beveridge noted 'the persistence, year after year, of high unemployment in some districts combined with low unemployment close by. Each locality has its characteristic level of unemployment, as each industry has ... There is no tendency, in any short period of time, for unemployment in different regions to reach the same or comparable levels by transfer of labour.'[24] Local variations are still in evidence. In the South-East, for example, unemployment in July 1982 ranged from 15·7 per cent in Chatham to 6 per cent in Hertford; in Scotland it ranged from 7·1 per cent in Aberdeen to nearly 24 per cent in Irvine; in Yorkshire and Humberside the lowest rate was 8·1 per cent in York and the highest 22·7 per cent in Mexborough. These variations were, however, far less extreme than in the 1930s and rather less marked than in the 1960s.

This does not mean that local differences no longer matter and that policies based on a 'territorial' approach to unemployment are now irrelevant. Recent research indicates, for example, that redundant workers' prospects of re-employment are more strongly influenced by the state of the local labour market than by their own personal characteristics.[25] Nor can we ignore the existence of exceptionally high unemployment rates in certain 'inner-city' localities. The causes of high, localized unemployment in large urban areas are well known. Firstly, since the 1960s there has been a general exodus of manufacturing industry from the inner areas of most industrial cities. Some jobs have been transferred to suburban or 'greenfield' locations; many others, particularly since the mid-1970s, have been permanently extinguished. Secondly, many small businesses in the distribution and service sectors have been destroyed by the combined effects of slum-clearance and road-development programmes. The disappearance of this type of unskilled, labour-intensive employment which traditionally absorbed many school-leavers and women has had a particularly marked effect on unemployment levels. As a result, although most inner-city areas have lost population in recent years, employment in these areas has contracted at a faster rate.

Despite attempts by successive governments to revive some

inner-city areas by improving the physical environment and inducing private enterprise to create more jobs, their future seems very bleak. Those groups for whom demand is particularly low and still falling – notably unqualified school-leavers and older, unskilled manual workers – tend to be over-represented in inner-city labour forces. In areas where there are large concentrations of Asians or West Indians unemployment rates tend to be even higher than in those where the labour force is predominantly white. In Bradford, for example, it was estimated that even before the start of the current recession Asian school-leavers had only half as good a chance of getting a job as their white counterparts. This reflects in part the heavy concentration of the Asian population in declining inner areas of the city and in part the marginal status of many Asian workers. In a recession such labour is particularly vulnerable to being both shut out and shaken out. It is hardly surprising, therefore, to find that between February 1977 and August 1982 Asian unemployment in Bradford rose by 330 per cent, compared with an increase of 240 per cent in white unemployment.[26]

The riots which broke out in the summer of 1981 in a handful of areas with large coloured populations must have further diminished the prospects of attracting more job-creating investment into such localities. It is hardly surprising therefore to find that over the years there has been a steady outflow of the more skilled and mobile workers from inner-city areas, leaving behind a workforce whose characteristics are less and less attractive to potential employers.[27] These supply-side difficulties are usually compounded by familiar physical and environmental problems; notably derelict land, vandalized and often uninhabitable housing and inadequate public services. If total unemployment was back to the average level of the 1960s and if resources for public investment in the inner city were far more plentiful, there *might* be a reasonable chance of at least halting the downward spiral. Since neither of these conditions is likely to be fulfilled, however, and since there are now many other towns and cities competing for jobs and investment whose supply-side characteristics are far more attractive than those of the inner-city areas, one can only take an extremely pessimistic view of the future of such areas.

## THE LONG-TERM UNEMPLOYED

It was argued in Chapter 1 that the bulk of those who enter
unemployment still succeed in leaving it within a relatively short
time. With the onset of the recession of 1979–80, however, the
outflow from the register fell relative to the inflow and the
average duration of unemployment spells increased. Many
workers who, prior to the recession, would have been assessed
as having 'good or reasonable' prospects of obtaining work found
themselves unable to get jobs as the familiar processes of shut
out and shake out began. Those employers who continued to
recruit labour were able to redefine and raise their standards of
entry. As a result, many workers who would otherwise have left
the register within weeks joined those who had already had relatively long spells of unemployment to swell the hard core of long-
term unemployed. In July 1979, for example, just over 24 per
cent of registered unemployed men had been on the register for

**Table 7    Long-term male unemployment by region (Great Britain)**

| Region | Percentage of men unemployed for 52 weeks or over | | | |
| --- | --- | --- | --- | --- |
| | July 1979 | As % of GB Rate | July 1985 | As % of GB Rate |
| South-East | 23·6 | 82 | 40·1 | 88 |
| East Anglia | 25·3 | 88 | 39·0 | 86 |
| West Midlands | 27·4 | 95 | 51·7 | 114 |
| East Midlands | 29·6 | 103 | 45·0 | 99 |
| Yorkshire & Humberside | 28·5 | 99 | 46·6 | 102 |
| North-West | 33·2 | 115 | 49·7 | 109 |
| South-West | 28·8 | 100 | 44·5 | 98 |
| North | 30·9 | 107 | 49·6 | 109 |
| Scotland | 30·8 | 107 | 45·3 | 100 |
| Wales | 30·2 | 105 | 47·7 | 105 |
| Great Britain | 28·7 | | 45·4 | |

(Source: *Department of Employment Gazette*, various issues.)

over one year, while 15 per cent had been on for between six months and a year; by July 1985 these proportions had risen to 46 per cent and 18 per cent respectively. Long-term unemployment increased in every region but rose fastest in the West Midlands, which also sustained the sharpest increase in total unemployment. Regional differences in rates of long-term unemployment, however, are far less marked than during the 1930s.[28] Would it therefore be reasonable to infer that the same factors which cause an increase in *total* unemployment also produce a rise in *long-term* unemployment? Over the postwar period as a whole, there is a marked similarity in the movement of these two indices, a similarity which has been maintained during the current recession (Figure 16). There are two other factors, however, which suggest that the problem has deeper origins. Firstly, the proportion of long-term unemployed in the total number of unemployed was gradually rising even before the current recession. Up to 1972 this proportion rarely rose above 20 per cent, whereas since then it has seldom fallen below this level.[29] Secondly, the characteristics of the long-term unemployed have in the past been markedly different from those of the short-term unemployed. Those on the register for over a year were much more likely to be male, old, unskilled and unqualified than those who moved into and out of unemployment relatively quickly. They were also more likely to have had health problems or some disability and a history of recurrent unemployment.[30] Only in some inner-city blackspots was the composition of the long-term unemployed at all similar to that of short-term unemployed.[31]

Since 1980, however, the increase in the average duration of unemployment spells has undoubtedly blurred, if by no means removed, the hitherto sharp distinction between the characteristics of these two groups. Long-term unemployment is currently being experienced by larger proportions of younger, more skilled workers who during the 1970s would have had relatively little chance of entering unemployment at all, still less of staying on the register for more than a few weeks. Regions and areas where unemployment was virtually unknown to the bulk of the labour force and which escaped relatively lightly during the 1930s have experienced sharp increases in both total and long-term un-

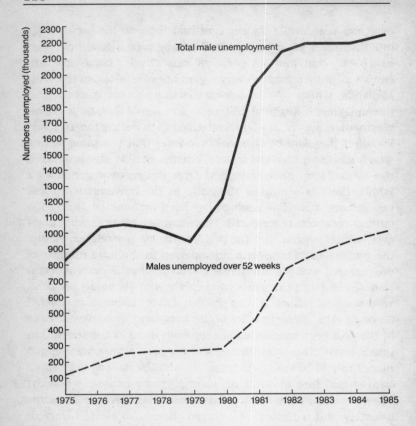

Figure 16   Male long-term unemployment: United Kingdom. (Source:
            *Employment Gazette*, April 1986.)

employment. It is therefore no longer sufficient – if indeed it ever
was – to seek to explain the existence of long-term unemployment
primarily in terms of the personal characteristics and deficiencies
of the unemployed. As Beveridge pointed out in his 1909 study:
'The fact that a man is inclined to be lazy or insubordinate or
irregular may be the cause why he rather than another is unemployed, though it is in no sense the cause of there being
unemployment. So the fact that a workman has been well trained
may cause an employer to prefer him to others and prevent his
being unemployed, without in the least affecting the total
numbers for whom there is no demand.'[32]

It is difficult to envisage a significant reduction in long-term unemployment without a *general* increase in the demand for labour. Training schemes and other 'special measures' may improve the employment prospects of individual workers and enable them to avoid prolonged spells on the register, but in the absence of an upturn in demand their success will only be someone else's failure. This does not imply a rejection of such schemes *per se*. On the contrary, they may well be essential if a large proportion of the long-term unemployed is to be prevented from becoming virtually unemployable. Even in the tight labour-market conditions which prevailed up to the mid-1970s it could never be assumed that most of those who remained on the register for long periods could not be placed in work.[33] There is certainly no justification for such an assumption in current circumstances. There is, however, a strong likelihood that a significant number of those who have entered the ranks of the long-term unemployed since the start of the current recession may *become* difficult, if not impossible, to place in employment even at a higher level of demand. Researchers have repeatedly emphasized the link between the duration of unemployment, the motivation to seek work and the prospects of getting it: '... there comes a point when people can no longer sustain their motivation in the face of continued rejection, heightened awareness of their own shortcomings, disillusionment with job-finding services, belief that all available options have been covered and a knowledge that jobs are scarce anyway. In short, people become locked into a vicious circle: lack of success in job-finding reduces their motivation and this subsequently reduces even further their chances of finding work.'[34] In regional and local blackspots where total unemployment has been relatively high for many years and long-term unemployment is, for a large proportion of the working population, a fact of life, there are now signs that this 'discouraged-worker' syndrome has begun to affect entire communities.[35]

## SUMMARY

In the 1970s the characteristics of the people who comprised the bulk of the unemployed were easily distinguishable from those of the labour force as a whole. The elderly, the unskilled, ethnic minorities, the socially disadvantaged and people with health problems were all heavily over-represented among the un-employed. These groups are still over-represented, but since 1980 the stock of unemployed has been swelled by school-leavers, men and women from the prime age groups, skilled and relatively well-qualified workers and people who live in regions and areas where unemployment has for a generation been minimal. The composition of those on the register for over a year has also become more representative of the workforce as a whole. It is, in short, no longer possible to regard unemployment in Britain in the 1980s as something which only affects 'particular people' in 'particular places'. Every age group, occupation and region has been seriously affected by the sharp rise in unemployment which began in 1980. Looking ahead, however, there is little doubt that the employment prospects of certain groups in the labour market will continue to decline relative to those of other groups. The demand for unskilled labour of all ages, male and female alike, will go on falling. Even skilled manual workers who are either unable to acquire new skills or have no opportunity to do so are likely to find their prospects declining. Cities and towns in the older industrial regions which have lost much of their manufacturing base over the past decade or so are unlikely to be able to attract or generate new forms of manufacturing activity, particularly in their inner areas. It follows that even if the econ-omy manages to sustain its recent rates of growth for several years, which many forecasters doubt, there will still be a clear need for governments to pursue policies designed to strengthen the employment prospects of the less competitive job-seekers and, where appropriate, to stimulate directly the demand for labour. The general response of policy-makers to the growth of un-employment is the next and final topic for discussion.

# CHAPTER 6

## STEPS IN THE RIGHT DIRECTION

*The world of work and business is undergoing constant change. To sustain the jobs our people want we have to respond positively to that change, and not to fight it. The price of failure to adjust and adapt is unemployment. We are paying that price now because over many years we adapted too little and too slowly. But a permanently high level of unemployment is not inevitable and our failures are not irreversible.*

Employment: The Challenge for the Nation
Department of Employment, March 1985

Is Britain stuck with its current level of unemployment for the foreseeable future, or is there a realistic prospect of reducing it? Looking at supply-side factors in the labour market, we can expect little assistance from this quarter. While the numbers reaching school-leaving age are projected to fall by about 20 per cent up to 1991, retirements and other exits from the labour force are also likely to decline. The combined effect of these trends will add about 0·5 million to the population of working age by the end of the 1980s, which will then remain broadly unchanged for the rest of the century. The implications for the size of the labour force, i.e. the number of people in work or seeking jobs, will obviously depend on activity rates but here again there is no reduction in prospect. Male activity rates are projected to stay broadly stable up to the end of the 1980s but female rates, as noted earlier, are likely to go on rising. What happens to activity rates thereafter will depend to some extent on the demand for labour, but it is difficult to foresee any radical change in these trends.

On the demand side of the labour market, industrial employment is likely to go on declining, although the rate at which it does so will clearly depend on the extent to which manufacturing industry, which accounts for about four-fifths of employment in this sector, succeeds in strengthening its international competitiveness. Given the British economy's dependence on overseas trade, job prospects in manufacturing will also be strongly influenced by the growth in world trade and by the competitiveness of the sterling exchange rate relative to other major currencies. If the recent fall in world oil prices is sustained, then the industrial world generally will eventually benefit from faster, non-inflationary growth and lower interest rates. Low oil prices, however, will also remove the cushion which North Sea revenues have in recent years provided for Britain's balance of payments and expose its dependence on manufactured exports rather sooner than official forecasts had been assuming. The need to achieve and sustain a major improvement in the competitiveness of British manufacturing industry is, consequently, all the more pressing.

But, say the optimists, both employment in the service sector and self-employment will continue to expand quite strongly and take up the slack left by a contracting manufacturing sector. This claim, as noted earlier, looks very dubious. Employment in the *public* service sector as a whole is now tending to decline and, given the sharper constraints on tax-financed expenditure implied by the fall in North Sea oil revenues, looks very unlikely to expand in the foreseeable future. The extent to which employment in the *private* service sector can continue to expand irrespective of the viability of manufacturing industry seems highly debatable. While it may well be desirable to encourage further growth in self-employment, it is difficult to see how this trend will make more than a marginal contribution to reducing total unemployment, while its relevance to the balance of payments is even less. The point is that the prospects for further expansion in service and self-employment depend fundamentally on the general rate of growth in the economy and, in the post-North Sea oil era, this will in turn rely heavily on the performance of manufacturing industry.

A strategy for reducing total unemployment must therefore focus on those measures, at both the macro and micro level of the economy, which are likely to help British industry to improve its international competitiveness. This must include all those factors on the supply-side of the economy, particularly the quality of the labour force, which have been identified as obstacles to industrial success. It also embraces measures aimed specifically at improving the efficiency of the labour market, the general objective being to reduce mismatches and improve the employment prospects of the long-term unemployed. While the present government would no doubt claim that it is actively pursuing such a strategy – a claim which is by no means without foundation – the seriousness of the challenge currently confronting Britain has yet to be fully recognized by policy-makers. The purpose of this concluding chapter is to draw together the various themes in the argument and suggest ways in which this challenge might be met.

First, however, we need to dispose of two beliefs which currently appear to be holding back a full policy response to the problems outlined above.

## WILL MANUFACTURING REVIVE AUTOMATICALLY?

In its evidence to the House of Lords Select Committee on Overseas Trade, the Treasury put forward an argument to the effect that manufactured output and exports will increase automatically to replace the declining contribution of North Sea oil to the balance of payments. Briefly, it starts from the proposition that the decline both in manufacturing's share of GDP and in the balance of trade in manufactured goods are part of a long-term and broadly inevitable process. In most other advanced industrial countries the proportion of GDP attributable to manufacturing, as well as the proportion of the labour force employed in manufacturing, has declined as the service sector has grown. The downward curve has been steepest in countries such as Britain, Holland and Canada where energy industries have expanded.

In Britain's case it is argued that the advent of North Sea oil merely accelerated the underlying deterioration in the balance of trade in manufactured goods. Since the balance of payments must balance overall, the replacement of a large deficit on trade in oil by a large and growing surplus meant, in the absence of a huge net capital outflow, that Britain had to export less and import more. Since manufacturing accounts for the bulk of both exports and imports it was inevitable that this sector (rather than, say, agriculture or services) would bear the brunt of the structural change. In addition, from mid-1981 onwards the economy moved into a cyclical upturn and, in common with similar upswings in the past, imports have risen faster than exports, thereby increasing the deficit on trade in manufactured goods still further.

Exponents of this analysis conclude that as North Sea revenues decline so the same mechanism will bring about a new equilibrium in the economy. They point out that the departure of North Sea oil (unlike its arrival) will be a gradual process, allowing much more time for readjustment. As the oil surplus declines the real exchange rate will fall and the balance on non-oil trade, including manufactured goods, will improve. Those manufactured goods, however, will not necessarily be produced by the same industries as in the past. Future growth opportunities are more likely to come from the high-tech industries which the Thatcher government believes it has done much to encourage. Income from overseas assets, which rose from £1·7 billion to £4·5 billion a year between 1979 and 1984, will also help to offset the loss of the oil surplus. Meanwhile there should be further development in the service sector of the economy, leading to a bigger net contribution to the balance of payments. Consequently the current deficit on trade in manufactured goods gives no cause for alarm. It will correct itself automatically.

NORTH SEA OIL AND THE EXCHANGE RATE

There are, however, several difficulties with this reassuring scenario. Firstly it assumes that there is a close relationship between oil and the exchange rate, when the evidence for such a relationship is by no means conclusive. It is worth remembering that although the prospective contribution of North Sea oil to the balance of payments was widely recognized in the mid-1970s, this did not prevent either the sharp devaluation of sterling in 1976 nor its maintenance at reasonably competitive levels in 1977 and most of 1978. If it was indeed the doubling of oil prices which drove up the exchange rate in 1979–80, when Britain was still in deficit on its trade in oil, it seems odd that the exchange rate should then have fallen in 1981 (particularly against the dollar) when domestic oil supplies were expanding strongly and the balance of trade was showing a strong surplus. Moreover the notion that both a higher exchange rate and a decline in manufacturing output were *inevitable* consequences of North Sea oil implies that it was the growth of oil production which brought on the recession in 1979–80 via a rise in the exchange rate. This in turn suggests that governments are powerless to manage the exchange rate and modify the impact of fluctuations in this rate on industry, which is of course contrary to the government's current policy. The high value of sterling in 1979–81 certainly hit manufacturing industry but it is very doubtful if North Sea oil was the main driving force behind it.

In its evidence to the House of Lords Select Committee the Bank of England suggested that only about a quarter of sterling's loss of competitiveness was due to the impact of oil.[1] The committee's own conclusion was that of the many factors influencing the exchange rate, the most important relate to *capital* flows rather than trade flows. Capital flows are in turn strongly influenced by changes in domestic interest rates and it is at least arguable that the appreciation of sterling in 1979–80 was the result of the government's own Medium Term Financial Strategy. Higher interest rates strengthened the capital account and a deeper than average recession temporarily improved the current account, the result being a sharp rise in the exchange rate. More recently, however, the government has fallen back on the exchange rate as a key weapon in keeping inflation down and has shown itself willing to force up the exchange rate by raising interest rates if its inflation targets are in jeopardy. This implies that if the Treasury view of the relationship between oil and the real exchange rate is valid, there will have to be a major fall in relative unit labour costs over the next few years. All recent evidence, however, suggests that this projection is implausible. In reality it is likely that the *nominal* exchange rate will have to fall substantially if the real exchange rate is to come down. If this is to happen, however, the government will be obliged to discard its current policy of keeping the exchange rate up in order to prevent a resurgence in domestic inflation.

## MANUFACTURING EXPORTS AND THE EXCHANGE RATE

A second major weakness in the Treasury's analysis is the assumption that currency depreciation will stimulate manufacturing output and exports to the extent required to fill at least a large part of the gap in the balance of payments left by oil. This in turn assumes that price competitiveness is the dominant influence over export performance. In reality, however, the task of improving British industry's market penetration is much more complex and formidable than the Treasury's analysis implies.

If a balance of payments constraint is to be removed by currency depreciation, then the demand and supply *elasticities* for both imports and exports must be sufficiently sensitive to produce a major shift of resources into export growth and import substitution. If, however, imports are price-inelastic, or if exporters respond to a falling exchange value of sterling by simply increasing their profit margins on existing goods in established markets, the necessary redeployment of resources is unlikely to happen. It is precisely such inelasticities of import demand and export supply which explain the failure of the sustained depreciation of sterling between 1971 and 1978 to effect a real improvement in the balance of trade in manufactured goods. One of the main conclusions which emerged from the investigations of the NEDC Sector Working Parties in the mid-1970s is worth quoting: 'Import penetration is now serious across large tracts of manufacturing industry. Despite price competitiveness, British exports in certain key manufacturing sectors are not proving very successful – because of poor marketing, lax delivery, or lack of expertise in sales and back-up services. There is a recognizable, if self-destructive, tendency for companies to stay in well-established markets, rather than try to break into new ones with much greater growth potential, particularly in the EEC.'[2]

Over the decade 1967–77 the price–quality mix of manu-factured imports increased, while comparisons of export–import unit values suggest that during this period British exporters were gradually being forced out of the expanding market for high-value-added, high-technology and relatively expensive manu-factured goods.[3] It was noted in Chapter 3 that the decline and disappearance of Britain's surplus of manufactured goods under-states a sharp deterioration in its trade with other advanced indus-trial countries such as West Germany and Japan, which in turn reflects an increasing concentration by British exporters on low-value-added, low-priced products.[4] Sectoral comparisons confirm this general trend. A study of British and German engineering exports in the mid-1970s, for example, revealed that the value–weight ratio of German machinery exports was about twice as high as the British in almost every product group.[5] This in turn strongly suggests that the superior export performance of the German engineering industry is based primarily on quality, design and technical performance rather than price.

Too much of Britain's export trade is, therefore, vulnerable to price competition from low-cost producers in the Third World and this vulnerability obviously increases with every percentage point that sterling is over-valued against a basket of competitors' currencies. When the sharp rise in sterling began to hit exports in 1979–80 the ministerial reaction was to argue that industry should compete more on quality and less on prices and must therefore move 'up market'.[6] This view, as noted above, implies a much more competitive performance in areas such as elec-tronics, where British companies face a huge disadvantage in terms of scale economies against their Japanese and American rivals and where Britain's overall trading deficit, already substan-tial, is predicted to increase to £4 billion by the end of the decade.[7] It will also require a major and sustained increase in the volume of investment in research and development, new manufacturing technology, better marketing and distribution facilities, retraining and so on. There is, however, no indication that investment on this scale is likely to happen. The recovery in manufacturing investment has been even more sluggish than

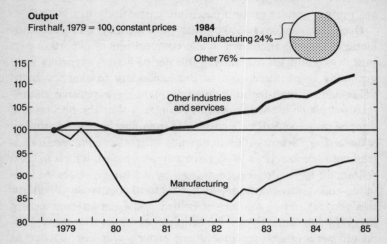

Figure 17    Manufacturing output in the UK, 1979–85. (Source: *Economist*, 5 October 1985.)

the recovery in manufactured output and, measured in constant prices, was at the end of 1985 still well below its pre-recession level (Figures 17 and 18).

Although this reluctance to invest has frequently been attributed by the CBI and other business organizations to the continuing high level of interest rates in the UK, a much more plausible explanation would emphasize the general weakness of business confidence and the low projected rates of return on investment in manufacturing assets.

As noted in Chapter 4, the average profitability of British manufacturing industry has been consistently low by international standards since the early 1960s and, despite some modest recovery since 1981, average returns are still too low in relation to alternative investment opportunities either in the UK or overseas. While other advanced industrial countries, including West Germany and Japan, have also experienced falling rates of return, the position of the UK has been and remains conspicuously weak. In these circumstances it is hardly surprising that a growing number of British-based manufacturing companies have been acquiring production and distribution facilities in overseas

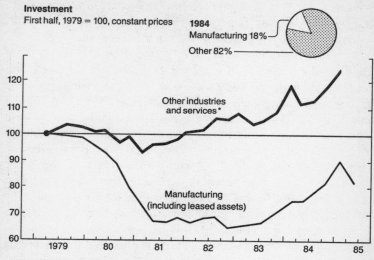

Figure 18   Manufacturing investment in the UK, 1979–85. (Source: *Economist*, 5 October 1985.)

markets. Such investment not only ensures their geographical proximity to foreign customers but also helps to reduce both their vulnerability to fluctuations in exchange rates and their dependence on relatively high-cost, low-volume domestic markets. For these and other reasons investment in overseas manufacturing capacity is likely to continue to yield a significantly higher rate of return than an equivalent investment in the UK. As long as this is the case it is difficult to see any substantial revival in investment in British manufacturing assets which is designed to expand capacity as distinct from saving labour.

## SALVATION THROUGH SERVICES?

The Treasury's apparent willingness to contemplate a continuing decline in the share of manufacturing in total output, employment and exports appears to be based on a belief that services will take up the slack. This in turn assumes that the growth of services and the decline of manufacturing are part of the same underlying structural transformation which is said to be characteristic of all advanced industrial economies.

A recent analysis by Gershuny and Miles, however, has challenged the conventional view that the output of services will increasingly supplant the production of manufactured goods as economies grow richer and more sophisticated.[8] They have argued that both goods and services are produced to meet the demand for 'final service functions' and, while the precise mix of goods and services is likely to vary over time, there is no inherent reason why services should be dominant in the long run. They cite the examples of the partial replacement of service-based transport (trains and buses) by the mass-produced motor car, the decline of cinema and music hall entertainment in favour of mass-produced televisions and video recorders, and the replacement of domestic servants by mass-produced labour-saving household goods. In each case a manufactured commodity has been able to meet the 'final service function' more effectively than a directly purchased service. It is this kind of substitution which helps to explain why, despite the fact that real personal disposable income in Britain doubled between 1950 and 1984, the volume of spending on services *fell* slightly as a proportion of consumers' expenditure. For any particular level of income, households are now spending proportionately *less* on services than twenty or thirty years ago.

There is in fact a strong incentive for entrepreneurs to design and manufacture goods which can substitute for previously-purchased consumer services. Over the past thirty years productivity growth in services has been much slower than in manufacturing, with the result that the price of services has risen twice as much as that of consumer goods. Consequently, while spending on luxuries may well increase as living standards rise, this relative price effect means that luxuries are likely to be embodied in tangible goods. One major reason for the continuing success of Japanese manufacturing industry is its success in seeking out profitable substitutes for services and mass-producing them to consistently high standards of quality and efficiency. In certain other Western countries, particularly Britain, entrepreneurs have been conspicuously less successful in this type of activity and in such cases the relative growth of service reflects a loss of dynamism in the manufacturing sector rather than a benign structural change.

Most of the growth in service employment since the early 1970s has come not from consumer-based activities but rather from public and producer-based services. In Britain roughly 40 per cent of all service employment is located in the public sector, which means that it is financed by tax revenues. Consequently it depends partly on political as well as economic factors for its future growth. The 1970s were, on the whole, relatively favourable to the growth of public service employment, particularly in education, which in the UK expanded by nearly 25 per cent between 1971 and 1979, and health services, which grew at the same rate. By comparison, employment in distribution grew by only 10 per cent over the same period, while in transport it fell by nearly 5 per cent. Since 1979, however, public service employment (except in health) has levelled off and even declined slightly. Much of the recent expansion in services is in fact attributable to the banking, insurance and finance sector, which in the UK increased employment by 19 per cent between 1979 and 1985. At least half of the two million jobs in this sector, however, are concerned with providing a range of professional services to industry and may be regarded as contributing in one way or another to the production of goods.[9] This type of employment, which is still expanding quite strongly, should therefore be seen as complementary to, rather than a replacement for, jobs in manufacturing.

The relationship between service industries and the manufacturing sector is essentially one of interdependence. It is consequently misleading to imply that the service sector as a whole can be expected autonomously to replace directly the contribution to GDP, the balance of payments and total employment which is currently made by manufacturing industry. Although forecasting the size of the 'post-oil' deficit on Britain's visible trade requires some precision about a range of uncertain variables, a recent middle-of-the-road projection made immediately prior to the sharp fall in oil prices in the first quarter of 1986 suggested that the non-oil visible deficit would rise from £11 billion in 1984 to nearly £24 billion in 1993 and to around £30 billion by 1995.[10] The reduction of roughly two-thirds in the price of oil, if sustained, is likely to cost the UK balance of payments between £2·5 and £3 billion in 1986 which, given the fact that the overall payments surplus in 1985 was only £3·5 billion, is of no small significance. Low average oil prices are also likely to reduce the output of North Sea oil and discourage the exploitation of new sources of supply. In short, the Treasury's previous assumption that the decline in North Sea oil revenues would be gradual, allowing the rest of the economy plenty of time to readjust, now looks increasingly unrealistic.

But, an incorrigible optimist might argue, even if the oil cushion is likely to be withdrawn sooner rather than later, will not services expand to fill the prospective gap in the balance of payments? This outcome seems inherently implausible. The magnitude of the task required to replace manufactured exports by services is illustrated by a sectoral breakdown of total exports (see Table 8).

In 1984 about 28 per cent of the UK's invisible credits came from exports of services and the bulk of the remainder from overseas investments which, as noted earlier, have increased sharply in recent years. Prospects for increasing the contribution from direct exports of services, however, are not particularly promising. Firstly, since many services are necessarily provided in close proximity to the end-user, the scope for international trade is much more limited than for trade in goods. It is currently estimated that only about 20 per cent of services are tradeable overseas.[11] Secondly, tradeable services are themselves subject to the same competitive influences as manufactured goods. Although Britain relies more heavily on export revenue from services than most other industrial countries, its share of world trade in services fell from 12 per cent in 1968 to just over 7 per cent in 1983, or slightly faster than its share of world trade in manufactures.[12] Moreover, the volume of services exports has been growing even more slowly over the past decade than the volume of other non-oil exports.

Nor should it be assumed that the large inflow of income from

## Table 8   UK exports in 1984

|  | £bn | % of total | % of imports |
|---|---|---|---|
| Food, drink & tobacco | 4·7 | 5 | 57 |
| Basic materials | 2·0 | 2 | 41 |
| Oils, fuels | 15·4 | 17 | 157 |
| Semi-manufactures | 18·3 | 20 | 99 |
| Finished manufactures | 28·3 | 31 | 89 |
| Others | 1·7 | 2 | 276 |
| **TOTAL VISIBLE EXPORTS** | 70·4 | 77 | 94 |
| Sea transport | 3·2 | 3 | 74 |
| Civil aviation | 3·0 | 3 | 118 |
| Travel | 4·2 | 5 | 90 |
| Financial | 2·8 | 3 | n.a. |
| Consultancy | 1·2 | 1 | n.a. |
| Students, diplomats | 1·6 | 2 | n.a. |
| Other services | 4·8 | 5 | n.a. |
| Government services | 0·5 | 1 | 34 |
| **TOTAL SERVICES EXPORTS** | 21·3 | 23 | 123 |
| **TOTAL EXPORTS** | 91·7 | 100 | 100 |

(Source: *Monthly Trade Statistics*, Department of Trade and Industry.)

interest, profits and dividends on overseas investment will continue at its present level. As the balance of payments moves into an increasingly large external deficit some of this investment will have to be 'repatriated' or, alternatively, the deficit will need to be financed by foreign borrowing. This in turn implies that interest rates in the UK will continue to be maintained at relatively high levels, which is hardly likely to encourage borrowing by industry to finance new investment – unless, of course, the emphasis of economic policy moves firmly in favour of expansion.

None of the foregoing argument is meant to imply that services are somehow inferior to manufacturing. Not only is the dividing line between these activities increasingly blurred but, to reiterate a point made above, there is a high level of mutual inter-dependence between them. An efficient manufacturing industry or company needs an equally efficient network of producer and distributive services, just as it requires a good educational service to supply it with an adequate number of qualified recruits. What the service sector cannot do is to *replace* output and exports lost by an uncompetitive manufacturing sector. Nor can it be expected to soak up much of the labour which will continue to be either shaken out or shut out of manufacturing. Un-employment has risen strongly in Britain over the past few years precisely because the service sector has only been able to absorb a very small proportion of the labour displaced by the contraction of manufacturing. New service jobs have been filled by women entering the labour force, often on a part-time basis. As a result women now account for 55 per cent of the service sector's labour force, compared with little more than a quarter in manufac-turing. The prospects for further growth in service employment will, as in the past, depend mainly on the general rate of growth in the economy and on the capacity of the manufacturing sector to create wealth.


## IMPROVING INDUSTRIAL COMPETITIVENESS

The perceived decline of manufacturing industry in Britain has aroused new interest, at least within the ranks of the opposition parties in Parliament, in the idea of an 'industrial strategy'. In general terms it is argued that industrial policy should be used both to provide first aid for uncompetitive but strategically important industries and companies and to apply longer-term remedial treatment. The focus is on changes, adjustments and responses within industry and on the role of government in stimulating them. Such an approach implies a generally more positive, interventionist stance than the Thatcher government has taken. The emphasis would move away from policy measures which are purely supportive in character towards those that are *simultaneously* supportive and innovative. This means that the government should be ready to commit more resources, possibly

at the expense of other items in the industrial support programme, to activities such as helping to finance industrial research and development, encouraging technological innovation,
providing long-term aid for promising but risky new ventures and
for necessary restructuring in the older industries, and assisting
companies with 'soft loans' to win major contracts in overseas
markets.

The idea of a positive industrial strategy along the lines described above, however, attracts considerable scepticism. Critics
argue that the problems of British industry are too deep-seated to
be resolved primarily by the provision of more generous packages
of financial support. They point to the record of government intervention in industry over the past thirty years and, quoting
examples such as Concorde, the civil nuclear power programme,
the formation of British Leyland and the selective support given
to the computer, machine tools, textiles and foundry sectors,
conclude that politicians and civil servants are not adept at this
type of decision-making. They also challenge the assumption
which underlies the concept of an industrial strategy that there
exists a well-defined entity (sometimes expressed as Great Britain
Limited) which has readily ascertainable needs, capabilities and
priorities. Any attempt to define these priorities by institutional
means, for example, through a system of top-level corporatist
committees operating out of Whitehall, is likely to substitute
political for market criteria in allocating taxpayers' money to
industrial subsidies. There is every likelihood, say the critics, that
a positive industrial strategy will simply add a veneer of official
respectability to measures which are fundamentally protectionist
and mercantilist in character.[13]

## THE THATCHER GOVERNMENT'S RESPONSE

The Thatcher government's attitude to the manufacturing sector
has been ambivalent. On the one hand some ministers appear to
believe that the decline in manufacturing is the result of relatively
benign structural change in the economy and that the role of
government is to encourage this process, not frustrate it by
propping up old, uncompetitive industries with subsidies, import

quotas and other protectionist measures. One specific manifestation of this approach is the government's declared policy of phasing out fiscal subsidies for manufacturing investment in order to make the tax system neutral as between different sectors of the economy. More generally the government has consistently given priority to reducing inflation by pursuing tight monetary policies. These policies have kept interest rates in the UK relatively high and maintained the exchange rate at a level which has damaged competitiveness in export markets.

On the other hand, some ministerial statements have occasionally implied a more positive commitment to improving manufacturing competitiveness. The government has continued to support industry in various ways and indeed, through the Department of Trade and Industry, has achieved a significant shift of resources away from purely supportive forms of expenditure (for example, automatic regional development grants and subsidies to nationalized industries) towards more explicitly *innovative* activities. Spending on research and development projects and on promoting technological innovation now accounts for nearly one-third of the direct support for industry provided by the DTI, compared with only 9 per cent in 1982. While emphasizing their unswerving support for free trade, ministers (including the Prime Minister) have become heavily involved in promoting exports, encouraging inward investment and pressurizing certain multi-national companies, particularly in the automotive industry, to buy more British-made products. More recently ministers have begun to grasp the nettle of education and training and appear determined to improve the capacity of the education system to meet the needs of industry. Thus, while denying that it has a 'strategy' for British industry, by which it means the top-down, corporatist approach which was briefly pursued in the mid-1970s, the Thatcher government would argue that its policies are designed to help industry to improve its performance in world markets.

While many industrialists would probably accept that the government is now broadly moving in the right direction, there is still a widespread feeling – particularly in the manufacturing sector – that ministers in general are still failing to recognize the size and urgency of the task. While accepting that it is basically the responsibility of management to improve the competitiveness of British industry, many industrialists argue that progress would be faster if this objective was firmly placed at the centre of all government activity and not seen as the exclusive concern of the DTI. The business community as a whole, however, has been slow to develop a clear and persuasive statement of what precisely it would like the government to do which it is not already doing. This reluctance in turn reflects considerable ambiguity in the attitude of industry as a whole towards the role of government in the economy. Few businessmen wish to be seen to be holding out the begging bowl for government grants and subsidies and most find it easy to unite on a platform of less public spending and fewer fiscal burdens on industry. Yet the demand that the government should 'do more' for industry in general, and manufacturing in particular, often translates itself into policy actions (for example, more spending on infrastructure projects, on support for technological innovation, on export promotion and on increased provision for training and retraining) which imply some *increase* in public borrowing and spending. If industry wishes to increase its influence over the policy-making process in Whitehall, irrespective of the political colour of the government, it will have to articulate the policy responses it requires rather more coherently than in the past. The following section attempts to sketch out a possible approach to defining these responses.


## A TOTAL APPROACH TO INDUSTRIAL COMPETITIVENESS

The only way in which British industry can improve its international competitiveness in the longer term is by achieving a much faster rate of innovation in its products and manufacturing processes. This is not simply or even primarily a matter of manipulating policy instruments such as fiscal incentives and project aid, although these may well have an important supportive role. Establishing a national commitment to innovation,

which will translate itself into faster economic growth, higher
living standards, better public services and, ultimately, lower
unemployment, means that all relevant resources must be organized with this objective clearly in mind. An approach to policy-
making which views innovation simply as a response to the
immediate pressures of the marketplace is an inadequate basis
for longer-term industrial success. It is this approach, tempered
by spasmodic bureaucratic intervention from the centre, which
has traditionally been followed in Britain, except in wartime. It
has produced one of the highest levels of unemployment and one
of the lowest standards of living in Western Europe. There is, of
course, no one single solution to the shortcomings in Britain's
industrial performance discussed earlier in this book. Achieving
a major long-term improvement in industrial competitiveness
requires fundamental changes in attitudes and practices across
the entire supply-side of the economy – hence the need for more
effective national organization and coordination.

It is difficult to see how this need can be met without some
change in the way in which successive governments view and
manage the economy. Without falling into the obvious trap of
advocating the establishment of a new super-ministry, it is clearly
unsatisfactory that the voice of industry in Whitehall – the
Department of Trade and Industry – is as weak as it appears to
be. By contrast the Treasury – which has traditionally controlled
the overall management of the economy – currently adheres to
the view that the decline in British manufacturing industry is
both inevitable and of no special consequence. Assuming that
this pernicious nonsense will one day be uprooted in Whitehall,
there is an obvious need to devise some means of bringing together all those ministers and civil servants whose decisions have
a direct impact on industry and who in one way or another
influence industrial performance and profitability. Once brought
together, this group would have the task of forming a longer-
term assessment of Britain's economic prospects, setting clear
objectives for improving its performance, and ensuring that the
general framework of fiscal, monetary and spending policies was
geared to these objectives. The re-establishment of a body
equivalent to the Central Policy Review Staff, mistakenly abol-

ished in 1983, would no doubt assist the development of a longer-term non-departmental view of the economy. Seasoned Whitehall-watchers will no doubt dismiss this suggestion as naïve and impractical, but unless some means can be found of communicating a sense of national urgency and direction to the task of improving industrial competitiveness, this overall objective will not be achieved.

For industrial policy-makers there are three factors which together have a major influence over both price and non-price competitiveness and, therefore, over the long-term rate of productivity growth. These factors are product innovation, process innovation and education and training.

## PRODUCT INNOVATION

The rate of product innovation is determined by the level and direction of spending on research and development throughout the economy as a whole. Research and development should be regarded in the same way as expenditure on fixed capital – that is, as an investment which will contribute to future output. The ability of industrial enterprises and public sector bodies to seek out new products and processes through research and development could, in fact, be seen as a major influence on the level and quality of fixed capital investment. Viewed in these terms, Britain's recent record in R&D gives cause for concern. Although, measured as a percentage of GDP, the volume of R&D spending in the UK is not significantly out of line with that of countries such as West Germany and Japan, the relatively poor international competitiveness of British industry implies that this ratio should be significantly increased over the next few years. In any case, broad aggregates tell us nothing about the direction and effectiveness of R&D expenditure and it is in these areas where Britain's comparative performance is really worrying. Roughly one-third of total R&D spending in Britain is financed by the public sector, over half of which is consumed by military, nuclear and defence-related projects. This reflects a far higher commitment to defence than in any other OECD country except the USA and its relevance to Britain's much-reduced world role is clearly questionable. Most ominously, spending on R&D by British manufacturing industry as a whole has actually fallen in real terms since the late 1970s.

How might this trend be reversed? Obviously the government could make a direct contribution by reducing the proportion of public funds currently absorbed by defence-related activities and switching resources into promoting collaborative industrial research projects which are likely to have major commercial applications in world markets. Such projects typically need to be sustained over several years and, as such, may be relatively unattractive to companies with limited funds for R&D and more pressing, short-term priorities centred on the development of existing products. The role of direct government aid is, however, at best that of a catalyst and facilitator. The real solution is to increase the volume and effectiveness of the R&D which manufacturing companies do for themselves. Traditionally this expenditure has been financed from retained profits which, in Britain, are still comparatively low. It may therefore be appropriate to consider introducing a tax credit scheme to encourage companies to increase their investment in longer-term basic research.

## PROCESS INNOVATION

Research and development has traditionally been associated almost exclusively with the design and development of new products. In recent years, however, it has become clear that in the manufacturing sector as a whole, product innovation is closely linked with the development and application of new production processes. 'Process' in this sense embraces not only the introduction of advanced manufacturing technology such as computer-controlled machine tools but also, and perhaps more importantly, the development of new methods of *organizing* the production process. The application of manufacturing control systems based on Japanese concepts such as 'Just-In-Time' has clearly exposed the potential which exists in many British factories for achieving step-changes in productivity *and* major improvements in product quality, together with much-reduced levels of indirect labour and stocks.

The rate of innovation in manufacturing technology and methods depends partly on the availability of internal funds but also, and probably more importantly, on the level of awareness among managers of the existence and benefits of these new techniques. There is still some evidence to suggest that many British managers are more inclined to rely on personal observation to keep themselves abreast of new developments in this field than are, for example, their Japanese counterparts. While one in four Japanese companies has a board member with special responsibility for technology, in Britain the proportion is one in thirty.[14] The Thatcher government has recognized that it has a role to play in spreading awareness within industry of these new technologies and techniques, but whether the relatively modest funds which it has committed to this objective will prove to be sufficient remains to be seen.

Could governments make a more direct contribution to accelerating process innovation in the manufacturing sector? Firstly, they could be somewhat less beguiled by the claims of the so-called 'sunrise' industries on the innovation aid budget and recognize more explicitly that the older industries, which already have significant markets outside the UK and employ relatively large numbers of people, require a bigger share of whatever aid is available. There is huge scope for improving the competitiveness of the mature industries (which are 'mature' only in the concept of their products) through the organized transformation of their systems of product design and manufacturing. The rate of progress will also depend, however, on the availability of manpower who are equipped with the skills necessary to undertake the redesign of manufacturing systems and, additionally, on the speed with which the direct-labour force can be trained and retrained to operate the new technology. At present most of the burden of training and retraining is being carried by industry itself and it is arguable that additional financial support from government would accelerate progress.

## THE QUALITY OF THE LABOUR FORCE

This brings us to the third factor which could undoubtedly improve the longer-term competitiveness of British industry, namely a substantial advance in the technical literacy and general adaptability of the labour force. The Thatcher government has, to its credit, become acutely aware of the relationship between the quality of the labour force and industrial performance and has taken several important steps to gear the output of the education system to the needs of wealth-creating businesses. Firstly, it is currently attempting to develop a school curriculum which provides a better foundation for subsequent training and employment. Secondly, the Manpower Services Commission's Technical and Vocational Education Initiative (TVEI) is designed to improve the quality of the education which those in the crucial fourteen- to eighteen-year-old age group receive in secondary schools and tertiary institutions. Thirdly, and more controversially, between 1983 and 1986 the Youth Training Scheme (YTS) provided up to one year's work-based training for over one million school-leavers. In April 1986 the scheme was expanded to give sixteen-year-old school-leavers a two-year place and seventeen-year-olds a one-year place. While this scheme is obviously preferable to letting thousands of school-leavers go straight on to the unemployment register, its success in assisting them to find permanent employment is clearly limited. The Manpower Services Commission is, therefore, actively seeking to ensure that all young people under the age of eighteen have the opportunity either to continue in full-time education or a period of planned work experience combining work-related training and education.

It is less and less likely, however, that the initial training which school-leavers and new entrants to the labour force receive, however good it may be, will last them a lifetime. The Manpower Services Commission has recently estimated that between half and three-quarters of the adult workforce will need some training or retraining over the next five years merely to keep pace with the demands of technological change. While the Commission acknowledges that it must stimulate and to some extent pump-prime training and retraining initiatives, the main responsibility for taking action has been laid firmly on the shoulders of employers. This approach clearly assumes, however, that employers as a whole will be prepared to give training and related activities a much higher priority than in the past. Since the weight of historical experience suggests that neither exhortation nor blanket statutory schemes (such as Industrial Training Boards) are likely to achieve this objective, new methods must be found. One particularly interesting suggestion is that an Industrial Training Credit system should be introduced. This would in essence give every employee a financial account which would cover the cost of an agreed individual training entitlement and to which both the employee and the employer would contribute. Both parties would therefore have an obvious incentive to ensure that the entitlement was fully utilized. Other practical proposals include using tax reliefs to encourage companies both to invest in training facilities and equipment and to donate more money to educational institutions.[15]

A higher level of direct investment by employers in the higher education system would undoubtedly help the universities and polytechnics to make their courses more relevant to the current and prospective needs of industry. It is very doubtful, however, if this alone will be enough to dismantle the barriers which in Britain have traditionally separated the world of advanced learning from the world of work. More central direction is needed in order to ensure that hitherto autonomous educational institutions redeploy resources in favour of research and teaching in disciplines which industry regards as directly relevant to the task of improving its international competitiveness. This is the corollary of a nationally prescribed curriculum in secondary education. It presumes a break with the tradition of local educational autonomy and a vigorous rationalization of existing course provision. It also envisages that the remuneration of lecturers and researchers who specialize in areas of skill shortage will reflect their relatively high market value. As in other areas, the Thatcher government has belatedly attempted to tackle the least progressive features of the traditional system but the pace of change needs to be quickened.

## ASSISTING THE UNEMPLOYED

The only effective way of increasing the capacity of the British economy to create the kind of jobs which will prevent a further substantial increase in unemployment and simultaneously get some of those who are currently unemployed back into work is by achieving a step-change in industrial competitiveness. The strategy sketched out above, however, will take several years to bear fruit and in the meantime the problem of long-term unemployment is likely to become even more acute. The response of policy-makers to this problem, however, has hitherto amounted to little more than a series of essentially cosmetic expedients and a more radical approach is now needed.

Long-term unemployment can no longer be explained primarily in terms of the personal characteristics of the unemployed and their geographical location. In recent years it has spread from the margins of the labour market to the core, from the old industrial regions to the more buoyant areas of the country, and from the older age groups to the young and those of prime working age. A comprehensive approach to reducing long-term unemployment must, therefore, focus on both supply and demand-side factors. Firstly, there must be more investment in training and retraining the long-term unemployed, a responsibility which rests squarely on the shoulders of the government and the Manpower Services Commission, albeit with some private sector involvement. This could, in turn, be linked, as suggested by the CBI, to the existing Enterprise Allowance scheme under which unemployed people are paid £40 a week for up to a year while they start their own businesses. If this scheme is made available to those taking recognized training courses to improve their employment prospects, possibly through a voucher system, it would both expand the number of new businesses and increase their prospects of achieving viability after the withdrawal of the first-year subsidy.

Secondly, since the employment opportunities for workers who have been on the unemployment register for over a year, even with the benefits of training and retraining, are unlikely to increase over the next few years – and may even contract further

– new opportunities need to be created by the selective use of public funds. New jobs can be created either directly, through schemes such as the present Community Programme, or indirectly by increasing publicly funded investment projects. The origin of direct schemes in Britain goes back over a decade to the ill-fated Job Creation Programme, which was succeeded in turn by the Special Temporary Employment Programme, the Community Enterprise Programme and – the latest variation on this theme – the Community Programme. The main and generally justified criticism of such schemes is that they involve relatively high levels of expenditure (for example, £460 million to provide 230,000 places on the Community Programme in 1986–7) but, beyond making a cosmetic reduction in the unemployment figures, do little to improve the job prospects of the workers involved. Many of the jobs created are unskilled and require little if any prior training; consequently they make little contribution to improving the stock of skilled and employable manpower. The best that can be said of these schemes is that by helping to sustain the work ethic they may also help to prevent the individuals concerned from becoming unemployable.

A much more effective approach would be to stimulate the demand for labour by increasing expenditure on relatively labour-intensive public or infrastructure investment projects. The need for this type of investment in Britain and the potential contribution it could make to reducing unemployment have been repeatedly urged by the CBI and other business organizations in recent years.[16] They point to the significant decline in public capital spending as a proportion of total government spending since 1979 and to the outward and visible signs of this trend – for example, the increasingly inadequate network of roads and motorways, the spread of urban derelict land, the huge and growing backlog of repairs and maintenance for schools and hospitals, and the abysmal state of the railway system.

In its 1986 Budget submission the CBI argued that additional capital spending of up to £1 billion a year could be accommodated within the Thatcher government's existing financial strategy and would be paid for largely by economies in public sector revenue spending. The government, however, has hitherto rejected the case for enhanced spending on the infrastructure on the ground that this would prejudice one of its major economic objectives, which is to reduce total public borrowing as a proportion of GDP. Additional capital spending by the public sector would, according to the Treasury view, 'crowd out' investment by the private sector and would therefore reduce the general rate of economic growth. The case for additional, selective capital spending is, however, much more persuasive. Not only would such investment bring unemployed construction workers back into productive employment, thereby reducing their claims on the Exchequer, but would also in some cases (for example, transport) make a direct contribution to improving business efficiency.

## DO WE NEED ANOTHER INCOMES POLICY?

The renewed inflation in British industry's unit labour costs has predictably encouraged further interest in the old familiar problem of restraining the overall growth in money wages. Very few of the ideas for 'reform' which are currently in vogue, however, seem realistic in relation either to past experience or to the current structural evolution of the collective bargaining system in the UK. In the private sector the consensus of opinion clearly favours an increasingly decentralized system of pay determination in which bargaining more accurately reflects the problems and prospects of individual factories and business units. It is not immediately obvious, therefore, how any strategy which is designed to impose more central control on the bargaining process from the top down is likely to find favour with the bargainers themselves. The call for some form of 'concerted action' by governments, trade unions and employers at national level implies nothing more than a reinstatement of the familiar ritual of 'toothless jawboning' which has been followed periodically in Britain since the early 1960s and has proved itself totally ineffective. By the same token, the more radical proposal that an 'inflation tax' should be imposed by the government on 'excessive' money wage increases would undoubtedly be viewed by most managements and trade union negotiators as a challenge to their ingenuity in producing pay settlements which avoided the tax while satisfying their own objectives.[17]

Any change in the established *mores* of pay determination in the private sector should be designed to help managements relate the growth of incomes more closely to the performance of individual businesses in line with the general drive for greater international competitiveness. The recent growth of interest in the wider application of profit-sharing schemes may therefore be seen as a potentially helpful development. Traditionally British industry has made much less use of profit-related bonus schemes than its American or Japanese competitors and there may be some conclusions to be drawn from such comparisons. Currently less than a million employees in Britain participate in some form of profit-sharing arrangement and the contribution which such schemes make to workers' gross remuneration is typically well under 20 per cent.

In order to encourage the wider adoption of profit sharing in Britain, the government would probably have to exempt profit-related bonus payments from employees' income tax or national insurance payments and, in addition, to stipulate that such schemes should relate a significant proportion of earnings to profits. The traditional argument against profit sharing, of course, is that most employees and trade union representatives would in practice be unwilling to accept the element of risk implied by the annual volatility of company profits. The evidence from the banking and financial sectors, where profit-sharing schemes are relatively common, suggests however that over a period of years risk-sharing could actually reduce variations in income.[18] The longer-term benefits for employees might also be emphasized by linking the amount of entitlement to bonuses to an individual's length of service with the company. Although there should be no illusions about the practical difficulties involved in bringing about the wider use of profit-sharing schemes, the potential gains to industrial competitiveness in terms of improving employee incentives and providing more scope for the non-inflationary growth of earnings can hardly be ignored.

## SUMMARY

It has been argued in the course of this chapter that the declining
contribution of North Sea oil revenues to the balance of payments
will not be offset automatically by an improvement in that of
manufactured exports. While further depreciation in the exchange value of sterling will to some extent offset British industry's poor performance in controlling its unit labour costs, the
problem of improving international competitiveness encompasses
a range of non-price factors which currency devaluation alone
cannot affect. Nor is it realistic to assume that the service sector
can directly replace a significant proportion of the exports and
employment which manufacturing industry currently provides.
Indeed, the reason why unemployment has risen so strongly in
Britain since 1979 is that the services sector, although continuing to expand its employment base, has not been able to
absorb most of the labour displaced so rapidly by manufacturing
industry. The relationship between manufacturing and services
is essentially one of inter-dependence. Much of the postwar
growth in the manufacture of consumer durables is attributable
to the substitution of those goods for services, just as the expansion of other services depends directly on the strength of
manufacturing. The future contribution which the service sector
makes to the total growth of employment will therefore be determined largely by the international competitiveness of manufacturing industry.

If British manufacturing industry is to increase its penetration of
export markets and simultaneously recapture lost business in its
own backyard, it must achieve a much faster rate of innovation in
both product and manufacturing technology. While the task of
achieving this objective lies mainly with industry itself, a more
overtly supportive role on the part of government could accelerate
its progress. The necessary changes would embrace the organization of economic management in Whitehall as well as the level and
distribution of government financial aid to both industrial research
and the application of new manufacturing technology. This is not,
however, an argument for a 'top-down', bureaucratic framework
of direct intervention. It is rather, in Ronald Dore's words,

a matter of providing sustained marginal incremental help to promising trends; of supplying organisations and mechanisms for feeding industry's expertise back to it; of helping to crystallise reasoned expectations about the future on which to base concerted action (sometimes, if necessary, primed by Government financial aid) designed to enhance the nation's competitive position.[19]

Nor is there a case for imposing central controls on pay bargaining in the mistaken belief that holding the growth of money incomes below some pre-determined 'norm' will either transform British industrial competitiveness or price a significant number of the unemployed back into work. The priority for policy-makers is not so much to push down money wages as to accelerate the growth of productivity. It is in this context that policy measures aimed at improving incentives for workers and managers alike, for example through the wider use of profit-sharing schemes, should be actively encouraged by the government.

It is not in the private wealth-creating sector of the economy but in the public education service that stronger 'top-down' direction is necessary. If British industry is to gain the major competitive advantage of being able to draw on a technically literate and adaptable labour force, some radical changes are needed in the philosophy and organization of every branch of the education service. Such changes are, as the Thatcher government has realized, unlikely to be achieved by relying on the traditional formula of exhortation and voluntary local cooperation. The priorities are to develop nationally prescribed primary- and secondary-school curricula which give more weight to the subjects appropriate to a science and technology-based society. Corresponding changes are also needed in the higher-education sector in order to increase the output of graduates in disciplines such as engineering and information technology. An improvement in the quality and number of graduates with skills and knowledge which meet the needs of industry is, however, only part of the solution. Industry itself must match the best practices of Britain's international competitors in training and retraining its existing workforce. The introduction of fiscal incentives may well accelerate progress in this field.

All these measures will help to prevent a further increase in long-term unemployment and should eventually reduce it. In the meantime, however, more action is needed to prevent people in this category from becoming unemployable. While make-work schemes such as the Community Programme can obviously make a marginal contribution to alleviating long-term unemployment, a more cost-effective method of bringing unused manpower back into productive work would be to increase spending selectively on public sector capital projects. Additional investment in training and retraining the long-term unemployed is also needed if their prospects of securing permanent jobs are to be improved.

The strategy outlined above will obviously make greater demands on the taxpayer's pocket than the present government's approach would permit. A policy, however, which gives priority to cutting personal taxation in an economy whose manufacturing base is uncompetitive is likely to achieve little more than a continued growth in manufactured imports. This in turn implies a further decline in industrial employment and relatively slow growth in the service sector. Achieving a step-change in the international performance of British industry requires far more than the prevailing economic orthodoxy suggests – indeed, nothing less than a total national commitment to improving the supply-side capabilities of the economy. The shock of the recession has initiated some encouraging signs of change but much more is needed – from governments, employers, trade unions and employees alike – if these are to be brought to fruition.

# NOTES AND REFERENCES

CHAPTER I

1. W. H. Beveridge, *Full Employment in a Free Society*, George Allen & Unwin, 2nd edn, 1960, p. 20.
2. ibid., p. 128.
3. See, for example, F. W. Paish, 'The rise and fall of incomes policy', Hobart Paper 47, IEA, 1969.
4. Beveridge, op. cit., p. 8.
5. *Employment: The Challenge for the Nation*, Cmnd 9474, London HMSO, March 1985, p. 1.
6. Speech to Labour Party Conference, reported in *The Times*, 29 September 1976.
7. James J. Hughes, 'How should we measure unemployment?', *British Journal of Industrial Relations*, vol. 13, November 1975.
8. John B. Wood, 'How much unemployment?', Research Monograph no. 28, Institute of Economic Affairs, 1972, p. 16. Wood argues that all unemployment which lasts less than two months should be 'deducted' from the unemployment register because it is likely to be frictional in character. There is no reason to assume, however, that all short-term unemployment must be frictional and therefore 'costless'.
9. P. C. Cheshire, 'Regional unemployment differences in Great Britain', NIESR Regional Papers no. 11, Cambridge University Press, 1973, p. 12.
10. N. Bosanquet, '"Structuralism" and "structural unemployment"', *British Journal of Industrial Relations*, vol. 17, November 1979.
11. W. H. Beveridge, *Unemployment: A Problem of Industry*, Longman, 1909, p. 41.
12. A. P. Thirlwall, 'Types of unemployment: with special refer-

ence to non demand-deficient unemployment in Great Britain', *Scottish Journal of Political Economy*, vol. 16, 1969.

13. R. C. O. Matthews, 'Why has Britain had full employment since the war?', *Economic Journal*, September 1968.

14. Maurice Scott and Robert Laslett, *Can We Get Back to Full Employment?*, Macmillan, 1978, pp. 16–17.

15. W. W. Daniel, 'Why is high unemployment still somehow acceptable?', *New Society*, 19 March 1981. See also 'Measuring unemployment and vacancy flows', *Employment Gazette*, June 1980.

16. 'Characteristics of the unemployed', *Department of Employment Gazette*, June 1977.

17. 'Fast service', *Employment Gazette*, August 1979.

18. G. D. N. Worswick (ed.), *The Concept and Measurement of Involuntary Unemployment*, George Allen & Unwin, 1976, pp. 119–29, 142–3.


CHAPTER 2

1. 'Jobs and Pay', *Midland Bank Review*, Winter 1984–5.

2. Olive Robinson, 'The changing labour market: the phenomenon of part-time employment in Britain', *National Westminster Bank Quarterly Review*, November 1985.

3. 'Why women want more jobs', *Lloyds Bank Economic Bulletin*, no. 83, November 1985.

4. Robinson, op. cit.

5. 'Labour force outlook for Great Britain', *Employment Gazette*, July 1985.

6. *Department of Employment Gazette*, August 1978.

7. Patrick Minford and David Peel, 'Is the government's economic strategy on course?', *Lloyds Bank Review*, April 1981.

8. David Metcalf and Ray Richardson, 'Labour', in A. R. Prest and D. J. Coppock (eds), *The U.K. Economy*, Weidenfeld & Nicolson, 1984, pp. 258–9.

9. 'Incomes in and out of work', *Employment Gazette*, June 1982. The authors added, however, that changes in taxes and benefits since 1978–9 combined with an improved take-up of benefits in work had probably reduced out-of-work

incomes relative to in-work incomes, 'in some cases substantially'.

10. This could well be the case among the long-term unemployed in this category. A survey by Research Services of Great Britain in 1979, for example, found that a quarter of its sample said that the relatively modest additional income they would get through working 'was inadequate compensation for the rigours of a job and the expenses incurred by travel and extra food' – Robert Taylor, 'The truth about unemployment', *Management Today*, March 1980.
11. Daniel, op. cit., p. 151.
12. W. W. Daniel, 'Is youth unemployment really the problem?', *New Society*, 10 November 1977.
13. *Employment Gazette*, June 1982.
14. W. W. Daniel, 'A national survey of the unemployed', PEP, 1974, p. 144.
15. 'The flexibility of the unemployed', *Employment Gazette*, January 1981.
16. Daniel, 1974, op. cit., pp. 42–51.

CHAPTER 3

1. W. H. Beveridge, *Full Employment in a Free Society*, George Allen & Unwin, 1960, p. 11.
2. F. Blackaby (ed.), *The Future of Pay Bargaining*, Heinemann, 1960.
3. A. W. Phillips, 'The relation between unemployment and the rate of change in money wages, 1861–1957', *Economica*, vol. 25, November 1958.
4. F. W. Paish, 'Rise and fall of incomes policy', Hobart Paper 47, IEA, 1969, p. 43.
5. Milton Friedman, 'Unemployment versus inflation?', Occasional paper no. 44, Institute of Economic Affairs, 1975.
6. P. Lilley, for example, has argued that 'the best guesstimate of the natural rate must be the average level of unemployment recorded over a couple of business cycles. Such guesstimates certainly indicate that the natural rate has been rising. It may well continue to do so' – Frank

Blackaby (ed.), *The Future of Pay Bargaining*, Heinemann, 1980, p. 58.

7. A. P. Thirlwall, 'Keynesian employment theory is not defunct', *Three Banks Review*, Autumn 1981.

8. J. A. Bispham, 'The new Cambridge and monetarist criticisms of conventional economic policy-making', *National Institute Economic Review*, no. 74, November 1975.

9. For an enthusiastic onslaught on the 'stupidity' of trade union leaders in Britain who have, allegedly, 'insisted' on 'extracting' higher and higher real wages for their members come what may see Lord Kahn, 'Thoughts on the behaviour of wages and monetarism', *Lloyds Bank Review*, January 1976.

10. *Economist*, 23 November 1985.

11. See, for example, D. H. Aldcroft and H. W. Richardson, *The British Economy, 1870–1939*, Macmillan, 1969.

12. R. Wragg and J. Robertson, 'Britain's industrial performance since the war', *Department of Employment Gazette*, May 1978.

13. Karel Williams, John Williams and Dennis Thomas, *Why Are the British Bad at Manufacturing?*, Routledge & Kegan Paul, 1983, pp. 13–14.

14. A. P. Thirlwall, 'Deindustrialisation in the United Kingdom', *Lloyds Bank Review*, April 1981.


CHAPTER 4

1. Robert Bacon and Walter Eltis, *Britain's Economic Problem: Too Few Producers*, Macmillan, 1976.

2. Walter Eltis, 'How rapid public sector growth can undermine the growth of the national product', in Wilfred Beckerman (ed.), *Slow Growth in Britain*, Oxford University Press, 1979, p. 121.

3. *Economist*, 12 November 1977.

4. David Stout, 'Capacity adjustment in a slowly growing economy', in Wilfred Beckerman (ed.), op. cit., p. 103.

5. 'Do we invest too much?', *Lloyds Bank Economic Bulletin*, no. 33, September 1981.

6. *The Margin of Spare Capacity and Constraints to Output Growth*, NEDC, 1977.
7. *Economist*, 9 June 1984.
8. *Economist*, 20 December 1975.
9. Harold Rose, 'Britain's financial system and economic performance', *Barclays Bank Review*, May 1982.
10. *Committee to Review the Functioning of Financial Institutions*, Cmnd 7937, London HMSO, 1980.
11. House of Lords, *Report from the Select Committee on Overseas Trade*, London, HMSO, 1985, p. 67.
12. *The Economist*, 14 July 1984.
13. Karen Williams, John Williams and Dennis Thomas, *Why are the British Bad at Manufacturing?*, Routledge & Kegan Paul, 1983, p. 35.
14. West Midlands Economic Planning Council, 'Industrial productivity – scope for improvement', in *Midlands Tomorrow*, no. 8, 1975.
15. *Economist*, 18 December 1976.
16. National Board for Prices and Incomes, *House of Work, Overtime and Shiftworking*, Report no. 161, Cmnd 4554, HMSO, 1970, p. 52.
17. S. J. Prais and H. Steedman, 'Vocational training in France and Britain', NIESR, May 1986.
18. S. J. Prais, 'Vocation qualifications of the labour force in Britain and Germany', *National Institute Economic Review*, no. 102, 1982.
19. *The Development of Higher Education into the 1990s*, Cmnd 9524, HMSO, May 1985, para. 1.3.
20. Martin J. Wiener, 'English culture and the decline of the industrial spirit, 1850–1980', Cambridge University Press, 1981, p. 132.
21. House of Lords, *Report from the Select Committee on Overseas Trade*, vol. 1, HMSO, July 1985, p. 51.
22. Keith Pavitt (ed.), *Technical Innovation and British Economic Performance*, Science Policy Research Unit, Macmillan, 1980, p. 95.
23. Coopers and Lybrand Associates, *A Challenge to Complacency: Changing Attitudes to Training*, Manpower Services Commission and NEDO, November 1985, p. 10.

CHAPTER 5

1. Jon Stern, 'Who bears the burden of unemployment?' in W. Beckerman (ed.), *Slow Growth in Britain*, Oxford University Press, 1979, pp. 78–9.
2. See W. H. Beveridge, *Unemployment in a Free Society*, George Allen & Unwin, 1959, p. 70 – 'Prolonged unemployment falls with crushing weight on the older men, once they have lost their niche in industry.'
3. W. W. Daniel and Elizabeth Stilgoe, 'Towards an American way of unemployment?', *New Society*, 12 February 1976. See also Daniel, 1974, op. cit., pp. 7–9.
4. D. I. Mackay, 'After the "shake-out"', *Oxford Economic Papers*, vol. 24, March 1972.
5. Beveridge, 1909, op. cit., pp. 116–17.
6. Colin Carmichael and Lois Cook, 'Redundancy and re-employment', *Employment Gazette*, May 1981.
7. W. W. Daniel, 'A national survey of the unemployed', PEP, 1974, p. 53.
8. See 'Characteristics of the unemployed: sample survey, June 1976' in *Department of Employment Gazette*, June 1977. Some 33 per cent of the unemployed in the over-fifty-five group with less than three months on the register were rated as having 'good, fair or reasonable' prospects of obtaining work; among those with over six months on the register the proportion fell to 13 per cent. The corresponding figures for the eighteen to twenty-four age group were 72 per cent and 46 per cent.
9. It is likely that part of the rise in youth unemployment in the mid-1970s reflected an increase in the propensity of young people to go on the register. This in turn was due to the combination of a rise in the school-leaving age (to sixteen), the eligibility of sixteen-year-olds to claim Supplementary Benefit and the effects of the 1975–7 recession on job opportunities for school-leavers – see *Department of Employment Gazette*, August 1978.
10. 'Labour force outlook to 1986', *Employment Gazette*, April 1981.

11. *The Economist*, 1 May 1982.

12. Chris Kaufman, 'Are the young really pricing themselves out of jobs?', *The Times*, 19 November 1981. There is evidence that since 1980 some employers have lowered their starting rates for young people because they have found themselves able to pick and choose between large numbers of higher-quality applicants for jobs. This, however, suggests that relativities may adjust to changes in the demand for labour, not the other way round.

13. Reported in *Department of Employment Gazette*, December 1977. These criticisms are by no means peculiar to British employers. A French employment-service official, for example, was quoted in a *Sunday Times* survey of youth unemployment in Europe (15 June 1975) as saying: 'What do you expect when the education system turns out youngsters totally untrained for a job or even for life itself? They demand well-paid work as soon as they leave school. What we need are youngsters conditioned to the hardships of life and the grim existence of the factory floor.'

14. As a result of this survey the CBI predicted that by the end of 1983 unemployment among the sixteen to eighteen age group would be running at about 75 per cent. In the words of Mr James Cooke, chief executive of the Special Programmes Unit of the CBI, 'We are confronted by a structural problem. Most school-leavers may not find regular work in the foreseeable future' – *Sunday Times*, 18 and 25 October 1981.

15. 'Is youth unemployment really the problem?', *New Society*, 10 November 1977; see also Daniel, 1974, op. cit.; some 45 per cent of the under-twenty-fives in this sample reported that they had been unemployed on two or more occasions in the past five years, compared with an average of 31 per cent for all age groups.

16. Beveridge, 1909, op. cit., p. 69.

17. Maureen Colledge and Richard Bartholomew, 'The long-term unemployed: some new evidence', *Employment Gazette*, January 1980.

18. Robert M. Lindley (ed.), *Economic Change and Employment*

*Policy*, Warwick Studies in the Economics of Employment, Macmillan, 1980, pp. 114–17.

19. G. C. Wenban-Smith, 'Factors influencing recent productivity growth – report on a survey of companies', *National Institute Economic Review*, no. 101, August 1982, p. 58.

20. Lindley, op. cit., p. 133.

21. Regional policy as it developed in the 1960s was based on the assumption that the prevailing level of unemployment was partly the result of the spatial mismatching of demands for and supplies of labour. Recent estimates of its impact suggest that it created about 100,000 jobs in the Development Areas; see Lindley, op. cit., pp. 150–53.

22. It has been estimated that roughly one million manufacturing jobs were lost in London between 1956 and 1981 – Tommy Macpherson, 'The decline and fall of London', *Management Today*, August 1981.

23. Nick Bosanquet, '"Structuralism" and "structural unemployment"', *British Journal of Industrial Relations*, vol. XVII, November 1979.

24. Beveridge, 1959, op. cit., pp. 61–2.

25. 'Redundancy and re-employment', *Employment Gazette*, May 1981.

26. Data supplied by Bradford Metropolitan District Council.

27. Peter Hall, 'The inner cities dilemma', *New Society*, 3 February 1977.

28. In June 1937, for example, the proportion of applicants for benefit who had been unemployed for twelve months or longer ranged from 7·7 per cent in London and 9·6 per cent in the south-east to 40·3 per cent in the north and 39·3 per cent in Wales. The average for Britain as a whole was 24·5 per cent – Beveridge, op. cit., p. 68.

29. J. L. Baxter, 'Long-term unemployment in Great Britain, 1953–1971', *Bulletin of Oxford University Institute of Economics and Statistics*, vol. 34, November 1972.

30. Colledge and Bartholomew, op. cit.

31. In inner Liverpool in 1976, for example, only 22 per cent of a sample of unemployed were over forty-five years of age, compared with a national average of over 50 per cent: 'High

unemployment shifts the burden on to men in the prime of life, among whom unemployment, in the country at large, remains relatively low' – Rupert Nabarro and Colin Watts, 'Looking for work in Liverpool', *New Society*, 20 January 1977.

32. Beveridge, 1909, op. cit., p. 134.

33. In a 1975 report the Department of Employment observed: 'There is no doubt that the register includes some people who might be described as "unemployable", who are exceptionally difficult to place and who seldom hold down a job for more than a week or two. These tend to be found among the elderly, unskilled or socially disadvantaged, and people who find it difficult to adapt to the conditions of working life. However, although some individuals are clearly more employable than others, it is not possible to draw a clear line' – 'The unemployment statistics and their interpretation', *Department of Employment Gazette*, March 1975.

34. Colledge and Bartholomew, op. cit.

35. A report in *The Economist* on unemployment in Sunderland (10 July 1982) observed that large areas of the city had adult unemployment rates of more than 50 per cent and concluded: 'In north-east England a culture seems to be appearing of dependence on government handouts ... Stolidly, the people seem to be settling in for a long period of freedom from the ambition to be employed.'

CHAPTER 6

1. House of Lords, *Report from the Select Committee on Overseas Trade*, vol. 1, HMSO, July 1985, p. 44, para. 80.

2. Robert Taylor, 'What the working parties saw', *Management Today*, June 1978.

3. *The Economist*, 27 May 1978.

4. Vivian Woodward, 'The British Dilemma', *Management Today*, March 1979.

5. D. K. Stout, *International Price Competitiveness, Non-Price Factors and Export Competitiveness*, NEDO, 1977.

6. *The Economist*, 28 July 1979.

7. House of Lords, op. cit., p. 45, para. 82.
8. J. Gershuny and I. Miles, *The New Service Economy*, Francis Pinter, 1985.
9. *The Economist*, 30 November 1985.
10. 'Manufactures in deficit', *Lloyds Bank Bulletin*, no. 85, January 1986.
11. House of Lords, op. cit., p. 43, para. 74.
12. Bank of England, *Bank Briefing*, September 1985.
13. 'Problems of industrial recovery', *Midland Bank Review*, Spring 1982.
14. Survey by PA Management Consultants, reported in the *Financial Times*, 12 October 1985.
15. Coopers and Lybrand Associates, *A Challenge to Complacency: Changing Attitudes to Training*, Manpower Services Commission and NEDO, November 1985, p. 20.
16. See, for example, CBI, *The Fabric of the Nation*, 1985.
17. Christopher Johnson, 'How to reduce wage inflation', *Lloyds Bank Economic Bulletin*, no. 84, December 1985.
18. Patrick Foley, 'Profit sharing creates jobs', *Lloyds Bank Economic Bulletin*, no. 89, May 1986.
19. Ronald Dore, 'Industrial policy and how the Japanese do it', *Catalyst*, vol. 2, no. 1, Spring 1986.

# INDEX

(Page references in italics refer to Figures, those in bold type to tables)